Hospitality: Sharing God's Welcome

Hospitality: Sharing God's Welcome

By Tammy Lindle

 Published 2006
Herald Publishing House, Independence, MO 64051

11 10 09 08 07 06 5 4 3 2 1

ISBN-10: 0-8309-1245-2
ISBN-13: 978-0-8309-1245-2

Printed in the United States of America

Contents

Acknowledgment

As I travel throughout the church, I have experienced the ministry of hospitality as both a blessing and an opportunity. It is a blessing to the extent that in many places, including homes, congregational facilities, campgrounds, work environments, God's welcome is most certainly witnessed. It is an opportunity yet to be realized in many other situations. As I share in missionary workshops, it is encouraging to note the number of people who recognize the need for a greater expression of hospitality in their congregations and desire to sharpen their skills in this area of ministry.

Hospitality: Sharing God's Welcome has been prepared to assist the individual disciple and congregation in reaching out to those who respond to an invitation or, on their own initiative, seek a sacred home. This resource helps lay the foundation for this critical dimension of personal witness and what it means to be a witnessing community. It is highly recommended for personal, small group, class, and retreat study and action.

Appreciation is extended to Tammy Lindle, missionary resource specialist, for her sense of call in researching and articulating the message of this resource. Tammy's own pastoral, missionary, and educational experience provides key insights into this witnessing opportunity. As it is used alongside *A Witnessing Community* and other related missionary resources, it is our hope and prayer that many will be blessed.

—Bob Kyser
Missionary Ministries coordinator

Dedication

I wish to express my deep appreciation to Gary Logan for graciously sharing his research and understanding about the true nature of hospitality with me. He has allowed me to partner with him in teaching and sharing. Through this kindness, I have become deeply aware of the power of sharing God's welcome through acts of hospitality. It is a precious gift of understanding—one I hope to perfect and pass along, first, as a way of honoring God, and second, as a tribute of gratitude to my friend Gary.

Chapter 1

Hospitality: Making Room in Our Lives and Ministry

There are many lives waiting to hear the redeeming words of the gospel, or to be lifted from hopelessness by the hands of loving servants. But they will be lost to you without the generous response of disciples who share from their own bounty that others may know the joys of the kingdom.—Doctrine and Covenants 162:7a

Heeding the Invitation

In the Hellenistic world, the peculiar way that early Christians practiced hospitality set them apart from the surrounding culture. Non-Christians prized hospitality, but understood it to be discriminate. It was directed toward family, friends, and influential social contacts—those who could easily reciprocate the host's goodwill. Christian hospitality, on the other hand, was notoriously indiscriminate. Not only were all welcome, but it was those least likely to reciprocate—the widowed, the orphaned, the outcasts, and the estranged—who were its primary recipients. In a modest way, Christian hospitality cut against the grain of social propriety and courted controversy in the ancient world.[1]

Early Christians talk about hospitality to the sick and injured, to the widow and orphan, to the sojourner and stranger, to the aged, to the slave and imprisoned, to the poor and hungry. At times it seems there is no class of people not included within the scope of hospitality. Perhaps that is as it should be, for there are many ways to construe "otherness," in terms of health, economic class, family relations, sexual orientation, nationality, age, or social status. The stranger status at the heart of Christian identity has biblical roots in addition to cultural and political ones.

Perhaps if the first step of living in hospitality is remembering who we are as Christians, the second step is recognizing who the stranger is standing before us. The stranger may seem suspicious or even dangerous. The very presence of the stranger can be disorienting. But if we look a little closer, we may see that our initial reading of the situation is wrong. Repeatedly, early Christian voices remind us to be prepared for surprises. The apparent stranger is not simply the poor, the stranger, the widow, the sick who knock, but Christ himself. Hospitality offered to another is always hospitality offered to Christ. In receiving others, we receive Christ. In rejecting them, we reject Christ.

It is important to examine and listen to the voice of scripture and, as Christian disciples, seek to understand the role of discipleship in a new way. Learning to look at the examples, expressions, and implications of hospitality as portrayed throughout God's word is a vital place to start. Connecting the scriptural foundation to our contemporary world and allowing that foundation to inform current practices enables us to experience discipleship in new and exciting ways. It in effect frees us to become bolder in our witness and outreach to others.

Scripture Focus—Matthew 25:31–46

31"When the Son of Man comes in his glory, and all the angels
with him, then he will sit on the throne of his glory. 32All the na-
tions will be gathered before him, 33and he will separate people
one from another as a shepherd separates the sheep from the
goats, and he will put the sheep at his right hand and the goats
at the left. 34Then the king will say to those at his right hand,
"Come, you that are blessed by my Father, inherit the kingdom
prepared for you from the foundation of the world; 35for I was
hungry and you gave me food, I was thirsty and you gave me
something to drink, I was a stranger and you welcomed me, 36I
was naked and you gave me clothing, I was sick and you took
care of me, I was in prison and you visited me."

37Then the righteous will answer him, "Lord, when was it
that we saw you hungry and gave you food, or thirsty and gave
you something to drink? 38And when was it that we saw you
a stranger and welcomed you, or naked and gave you cloth-
ing? 39And when was it that we saw you sick or in prison and
visited you?"

40And the king will answer them, "Truly I tell you, just as
you did it to one of the least of these who are members of my
family, you did it to me."

41Then he will say to those at his left hand, "You that are
accursed, depart from me into the eternal fire prepared for the
devil and his angels; 42for I was hungry and you gave me no
food, I was thirsty and you gave me nothing to drink, 43I was a
stranger and you did not welcome me, naked and you did not
give me clothing, sick and in prison and you did not visit me."

44Then they also will answer, "Lord, when was it that we
saw you hungry or thirsty or a stranger or naked or sick or in
prison, and did not take care of you?"

45Then he will answer them, "Truly I tell you, just as you
did not do it to one of the least of these, you did not do it to

me.' [46]And these will go away into eternal punishment, but the righteous into eternal life."

Consider the exchange found in Matthew 25:31–46. Jesus is sorting those who generously gave to the thirsty, stranger, naked, sick, and imprisoned from those who did not extend the hospitable hand of caring. Those who offered kindness to others are blessed and invited to "Come...inherit the kingdom prepared for you from the foundation of the world" (Matthew 25:34). Those who neglected to show kindness, Jesus ordered to "depart from me into the eternal fire" (Matthew 25:41).

According to Matthew's Gospel, concrete acts of righteousness on behalf of others are seen as central to obedience to Jesus' commands; and obedience to Jesus' commands is essential to salvation. Perhaps all of Jesus' disciples need to consider why Matthew's testimony to Jesus calls our attention to the stranger. Deeper still, why does this text connect aspects of salvation to the extent to which we welcome and serve the stranger in our midst?

Hospitality is best expressed in genuine acts of love and caring. We are best at being a host when the desire to offer our gifts and resources comes naturally, as a heartfelt response. However, for those who need convincing of its importance, the rewards and punishments related in Matthew's Gospel make it clear what Jesus' expectation is of his disciples. Beginning to recognize "when, where, and how" to offer gifts of hospitality is supported by understanding the basic "why" of sharing those gifts. Jesus says our salvation is connected to those acts.

The stranger is not simply one who needs us. We also need the stranger. We need the stranger if we are to know Christ and serve God. For the stranger represents possibilities in our own lives that we want to avoid facing. We do not want to look at the hungry and naked and homeless because we fear falling into those calamities ourselves. We avoid the stranger because he or she reminds us that we ourselves are strangers to others.

Reflection

- In what ways do Jesus' words in Matthew 25 help us understand our Christian discipleship?
- How should congregational life be structured to provide for welcoming activities?
- What implications does this scripture have for you individually regarding hospitality to strangers?

Hospitality As Lifestyle

The most common aspects of hospitality begin with attention to the basic physical needs of food and shelter. Sharing food with another person can be powerful. As a symbol it goes beyond the simple act of obtaining nourishment. Eating together can be symbolic of sharing life itself.

Beyond concern for meeting physical needs, true hospitality also includes care for social needs. When we help someone feel welcome, we are caring for social needs. By including an outsider or someone new within our friendship circles or within groups of associates, at a basic level we are recasting social relationships. This act of welcoming requires more than food and drink. "Acts of inclusion and respect, however small, have the potential to powerfully reframe social relationships and engender welcome."[2]

Other aspects of hospitality encompass spiritual needs. Sometimes this means including the stranger in worship. "Hosts can attend to the spiritual needs of guests through listening to their stories or receiving them into the larger community."[3] In early Christian texts, aspects of prayer focus on hospitality as an acknowledgment of the common dependence of both host and guest on God for everything. Prayers for healing and safe travel occur frequently, as do prayers of gratitude.[4]

One does not have to spend too much time in Bible study to pick up on the fact that hospitality is a high priority to God. Offering hospitality is central to many of the stories and teachings found throughout the Bible. Through them, we learn that hospitality is extended in a variety of ways in sharing simple meals or opening our homes, lives, and all that we have to unknown strangers. Many stories of hospitality contain elements of mystery and surprise because God is so often present in unexpected ways.

Many stories have their roots in scripture—stories of food that multiplied miraculously or appeared just when needed; people who came unexpectedly and brought exactly the skills required that day; risky situations that turned out to be filled with blessings. Each of these accounts of giving required an act of obedience and a generous trusting when someone offered up part of God's blessings for the benefit of another.

Because hospitality is a basic expectation for followers of Jesus, every aspect of our lives can be touched by its practice. In essence, it lays claim to the entirety of our lives. If we use hospitality as a lens through which to examine our homes, churches, jobs, schools, health care, and politics, how might we see them differently? How can we make the places that shape our lives and where we spend our days more hospitable? Perhaps we might ask how our current practices in these settings shut out those who are strangers. In what ways do our daily practices succeed or fall short of the expectations of Matthew 25:31–46?

Hospitality is a skill and a gift, but it is also a practice that flourishes as multiple skills are developed, as particular commitments and values are nurtured, and as certain settings are cultivated. And because hospitality is a way of life, it must be cultivated over a lifetime. We do not become good at hospitality in an instant; we learn it in small increments of daily faithfulness.

Hospitality is central to Christian identity. It is a fundamental practice of the Christian life, though it is frequently crowded out by other responsibilities and priorities. Challenges to grow in hospitality can feel overwhelming when we imagine adding one or more tasks to schedules that are already too full.

A first step in making a place for hospitality may be to make room in our hearts. Whether or not we can always find room in our houses, welcome begins with dispositions characterized by love and generosity. Our ability to open ourselves can be enhanced by praying that God will give us eyes to see the many opportunities around us, and by putting ourselves in places where we are likely to encounter strangers in need of welcome. We should not have to look too far to recognize strangers among us.

Hospitality is not so much a task to be accomplished and checked off a list as it is a way of living our lives and of sharing ourselves. Hospitality grows out of an attempt to be faithful to God, to hear God's voice in the scriptures and in the people around us. Our call as Christian disciples is to allow God's voice to be heard in the world, to be the hands and feet of Jesus—opening our hearts and reaching out our hands.

Hospitality as Ministry

In the early church, hospitality was an essential part of Christian identity. Welcome, compassion, and equal treatment were all part of a proper Christian response to people in need. Personal hospitality broke down some of the social barriers that were so powerful in the culture. However, over the centuries the scope of hospitality as a term or word has diminished. For many it now chiefly refers to the entertainment of one's friends and acquaintances and to the hospitality industry's provision of service through hotels and restaurants. The expectations and services once offered by the people of God have in many respects been sidelined away from the responsibility of the church through hotels, hostels, hospices, hospitals, and other social service organizations. Losing this distinction has weakened our understanding of our Christian calling, and allowed many of us to view care and welcoming of strangers as optional.

Scripture makes it clear that hospitality is not optional for the disciple. Hospitality is not first a duty and responsibility; it is first a response of love and gratitude for God's love and welcome to us. Although it involves responsibility and faithful performance of duties, hospitality emerges from a grateful heart. By definition, hospitality involves some space into which people are welcomed, a place where unless the invitation is given, the stranger would not feel free to enter.

Making people feel welcome and "at home" is not the same as entertainment. To offer Christian hospitality we will need to rethink and reshape our priorities. Hospitality will not occur in any significant way in our lives or congregations unless we give it purposeful attention.

Because the Community of Christ embraces respect for the worth of all people, and a belief that each of us, as members of Christ's body, is called to Christ's mission, hospitality as a vital ministry of the church should be embraced by each one of us. This is not simply a duty of the priesthood or those traditionally involved in women's ministry. It is not just a matter of offering greeting, a cup of coffee, or a bulletin as we show a guest to the sanctuary for worship. It includes those things, but involves so much more. Hospitality as a basic calling is given to each of us. And the expression of those gifts will be as varied and as individual as we are.

Each Disciple and Congregational Family Is Called

The practice of hospitality is not one option among several that Christians can choose to act on. What God has done and is doing for the world through Jesus Christ needs to be shared with as many people as possible, as often as possible, in as many ways as possible. Hospitality is the work of all the people working together. It is not the prerogative of the priesthood. It is baptism, not ordination, that gives a Christian authority for the work of this ministry.

Christian disciples and families in the congregation need to be reminded of the promise that was made at baptism. The covenant we made to be Christ's disciple is still binding. That covenant was made with Jesus, whose very entrance into human life did not meet with even a modest standard of hospitality. However, we must remember that the One born in a barn keeps the door open for each of us.

> **There is no room for Joseph and Mary in the town caravansary, the place where travelers would normally find lodging. So Mary gives birth to her child *outside* the town, the added detail about laying him in a manger suggesting a barn or stall for the housing of animals. This "visitor from on high" finds no "room," no hospitality...His birth takes place on the margins, beginning a pattern to be realized over and over in his life and ministry. The visitor from God, who could not find hospitality in his own city, will nonetheless institute in the world the hospitality of God. The poor, marginalized shepherds of Bethlehem will be the first to experience it.**[5]

The practice of hospitality won't transform our congregations if it is viewed as only one more in a series of programs to strengthen the church. The majority of the congregation must, at a fundamental level, come to feel that hospitality is a core part of their responsibility as Christians and come to share a vision of the congregation as a truly welcoming place. Hospitality is not a church-growth strategy as such. One does not practice hospitality in order to make the church grow. The emphasis with hospitality is on the other, the stranger, not on the growth of the organization extending the hospitality and not even on the needs of the individual serving as host.

We need to be reminded that hospitality is not simply the "good manners" that hold the door open for the guest and direct the way to the adult church school class. It is recognition that no matter how good it feels to be "at home" in our community of faith, we cannot enjoy intimacy among ourselves at the exclusion of creating space for the stranger.

For many people church is the one place, other than among the family, where they experience the warmth of being welcomed homc. People there know us and we know them, or at least a significant number of them. They are glad to see us, as we are glad to see them. We exchange news, catch up with one another's lives, support one another in common tasks and in times of need. The essence of hospitality is to be known and welcomed, needed and loved. However, so many of us in the church have lost the ability to be objective. We have become "church blind." We are either preoccupied with our place or task in the congregation, or have simply been a member and active participant for so long that we assume our experience of the friendliness of the congregation is, or ought to be, everyone's experience.

The Christian congregation is absolutely unique in that it exists primarily for those who are not yet members of it. This is a hard thing for long-time members to understand or remember. Of course the church is for members, too, but not to the exclusion of others. It is due to this fact that hospitality should not be sidelined to a small committee's responsibility.

Hospitality is not a task to be assigned to a committee. It is not maintenance but ministry, and thus the work of the whole church. Hospitality that is biblically informed and guided is not a public relations strategy to encourage church growth but a congregational lifestyle, chosen in order to be obedient to God's vision for the church.

Hospitality is also not an end in itself. The congregation's primary task includes reaching out to people, receiving them into fellowship, providing opportunities for them to grow in their relationship with God, nurturing them in faith, and sending them out to serve. The role of hospitality is to create an environment in which this flow moves without barriers or constraints.

This flow can be expressed in three movements: (1) welcoming ministries, in which the stranger is reached out to and received as an honored guest; (2) belonging ministries, in which the guest is incorporated into the community and becomes a member of the church family; and (3) discipling ministries, in which the new member, through teaching, prayer, fellowship, and service, is taught and incorporated into the community of God and sent out to serve.[6]

However, hospitality remains no more than good etiquette when practiced only among look-alikes, kindred spirits, and members of the club. In a world of vast diversity, every one of us has at times experienced life as an outsider in one realm or another. We know the discomfort, insecurity, loneliness, anxiety, and, sometimes, even fear that pervade an outsider's days.

The Community of Christ is focused on the practice and principle of sharing—sharing our resources and our witness with others. The instruction is consistent and clear. Encouragement has been provided as individuals and congregations have been empowered to share with neighbors and strangers. Stories offering support and highlighting successes are surfacing from areas where missionary efforts to invite, welcome, and nurture seekers and guests are being practiced in witnessing communities. This call to serve others is the call we each have as disciples. It is echoed in scripture, song, and story. The call is from Jesus. We hear it and claim it as our own, for our day, for our time, and our ministry.

Congregations need to honestly consider how they welcome guests, members, and especially strangers. When was the last time a guest was welcomed? Whose role is it to welcome guests? How does that welcome take place? An honest examination of these questions will take congregation members on a journey of discovery that, for some, may raise questions about their right to claim to be Christians. For others, new insights will be gained about just who the guest is and how often we are presented with opportunities to offer a Christlike welcome.

Learning to see the stranger as part of God's family will serve our discipleship in increasingly amazing ways. Our actions or inactions reflect what we truly believe. We should ask, "How can I best reflect Jesus' welcome to others? How can I keep in mind that the church exists primarily for those who are not yet part of it? What will I do to extend Christ's welcome through my life and my congregation?"

Through our searching and asking, we can expect that answers will emerge that will inform and guide our actions. We must take care to look closely at the examples given to us through scripture. These texts—both ancient and new—offer profound insight to disciples seeking to do God's will today. We must listen and respond.

> **From the earliest days you have been given a sacred principle that declares the inestimable worth of all persons. Do not forget. The One who created all humankind grieves at the shameful divisions within the hu-**

man family. A prophetic people must work tirelessly to tear down walls of separation and to build bridges of understanding. You hold precious lives in your hands. Be gentle and gracious with one another. A community is no stronger than the weakest within it. Even as the One you follow reached out to those who were rejected and marginalized, so must the community that bears his name.—Doctrine and Covenants 162:6 a–c

Sharing Our Story
Andy Shelton—Novato, California

As I was walking through the airport in January 2005, just having returned from Christmas vacation, I passed a bank of newspaper vending machines. My eye caught the headline, and as I got closer to the machine, I read that a student at the high school near my congregation had been murdered outside a restaurant in a nearby city on New Year's Day. I made a mental note of it, wanting to make sure I mentioned it during the prayers of the people at church the following Sunday. Little did I know at the time how close to home the story was for our congregation.

Several years ago the Novato congregation saw that there were several needs in the neighborhood and decided to respond to one of them by offering free English as a Second Language courses for the immigrants who live in the area. As a result, much of our outreach work has been with Latino families.

The morning after I got home, Prema, one of the Latina leaders in the neighborhood, called me. She told me that Jackie, the mother of the murdered boy I had read about the day before, was her close friend. Prema had been staying with Jackie since the murder and asked me to accompany them to the funeral as additional moral and emotional support. The funeral was to be held at Jackie's ex-husband's church, and she, herself, didn't have a pastor at the time. I said yes, of course I would go with them.

The funeral was on a Sunday afternoon. At church that morning I shared what little I knew about Jackie's story with the congregation, and we prayed for her. Later that afternoon, when I arrived at the funeral, the church was filled to overflowing with the boy's family and friends. The grief was palpable. I found Prema and Jackie at the front of the nave, and went to be with them during the service. It wasn't until the funeral was over that I had a chance to actually meet Jackie, though it was clear to me from the moment I saw her that she was overwhelmed by the loss of her son. I introduced myself to her, told her that I was a pastor of a church near her home, gave her my card, and told her to call me if there was anything I could do for her. She asked me for my prayers, and for the prayers of my congregation, and thanked me for coming. I told her that the congregation had already prayed for her, that I had shared with them that very morning about her son's death. She was moved to tears to know that a group of people she had never met had been praying for her.

A few weeks later, when Jackie felt emotionally strong enough, she came to church with Prema. The Novato congregation did what they always do: they make newcomers feel welcome, and since they knew about Jackie's recent tragic loss, they were especially thoughtful in the way that they welcomed her. Someone sat with her to help her find her way through the hymnal, and others sat with her during the refreshments we have after each service. When it came time for people to share their joys and prayer concerns, Jackie stood, and through a tearful voice, thanked the congregation for their prayers.

Jackie came to church several times until she had to move out of her apartment. One of the elders of the congregation mobilized a group of people to help her move, and although she lives too far away from the church to attend regularly, we still hear from her occasionally. She is thankful for the refuge the Novato Community of Christ offered her during the lowest moments of her life, and I am grateful to be part of a congregation that welcomes strangers and makes them feel at home.

Practical Helps for Congregations

Consider the following suggestions. Make note of one or two that your congregation can work to implement in the coming weeks.

- Marketing ideas for churches can be found through a simple Internet search. Care should be taken to assess theological compatibility before relying on any tool. A place to start for marketing ideas is *outreachmarketing.com.*
- Encourage people to serve where they have gifts and passion. Make spiritual gifts inventories or ministry skill assessment tools available and then make use of the results. An updated version of the *Discover and Share Your Gifts* inventory can be found at the back of this resource. Additional spiritual gifts analysis can be found at the following Web sites: *www.churchgrowth.org, http://mintools.com/spiritual-gifts-test.htm*, or *www.kodachrome.org/spiritgift*.
- Understand that Christian service occurs through vehicles other than church programs. Empower people to serve in ministry beyond the church building.
- Prepare a comprehensive listing of congregational ministry opportunities with descriptions and contact information. Keep it up-to-date.
- Create an attractive flyer or "one pager" for each ministry that tells its story and how to get connected.

- Lift up a different ministry in worship from time to time, celebrating its accomplishments and recognizing participants.
- Tell the story of what your church is doing together in ministry. Document activities with photos and journals. These can serve as reminders for where you've been and accomplishments made.
- Appoint a "chaplain" or "pastor" to watch over children and youth activities.
- Invite kids and parents to take part in church activities. Look for opportunities to build personal relationships with the families.
- Have each Sunday school class choose a mission project to support on an ongoing basis.
- Divide hospitality tasks among various groups and members of the congregation.
- Connect kids with the church's overall missional efforts.
- Teach that hospitality is at the core of the gospel.
- Teach your congregation to honor each person and help them understand that God seeks to be in relationship with all people.
- Convey a clear invitation and a statement of welcome in all communications directed at the external community.
- Gather feedback on how visitors respond to your church through surveys, focus groups, or interviews.
- Provide training on welcoming and greeter ministry at least once a year.
- Send members of the welcoming team to visit other churches. Have members report on their experience.
- Conduct a congregational "welcome audit" by drafting a guest survey. Two samples are included at the back of this resource, starting on page 144.
- Have music playing outside the church as a way to welcome people to the facility.

- Review the schedule and format of current church activities and events. Try new approaches that might appeal to those not yet active, for example, weekday breakfasts, downtown lunch gatherings, weekend retreats, etc.
- Relationships are key. Most people get involved and serve because they are asked. Personal invitations are the most effective method of getting someone involved. Be specific with a request and extend a personal invitation to respond.
- Make getting connected easy. Create easy entry points—short-term service opportunities requiring a minimal commitment.
- Have an intentional system that helps all new attendees and members become involved in groups and activities very soon after they start coming to church.
- Remember that choirs, service teams, and even administrative committees are also "small groups." Train leaders to make these experiences spiritually formative, rather than exclusively task oriented.
- Follow-up is important. Follow up with members periodically to ask how things are going.
- Recognize that sometimes people need a break. Give permission to say no when necessary.
- Care for your building and grounds as a way of honoring guests and members and honoring God. A well-cared-for building demonstrates a commitment to excellence and communicates that what the church does is important.
- Provide clear exterior and interior signage that guides a visitor everywhere he or she might need to go.
- Reserve special parking places for guests and those with special needs. Encourage members to park offsite or in more remote spaces.
- Make your nursery clean, safe, sanitary, well-equipped,

and visually appealing to children and their parents. Use a space that is easy to find and convenient to the sanctuary. Make sure your nursery workers are registered children and youth workers.

- Make sure restrooms are neat, clean, and well-stocked. Consider providing a few "extras" in the restroom facilities (Kleenex, baby wipes, hand lotion, seat protector sheets).

Chapter 2

Remembering the Tradition: A New Look at an Ancient Practice

Open your hearts and feel the yearnings of your brothers and sisters who are lonely, despised, fearful, neglected, unloved. Reach out in understanding, clasp their hands, and invite all to share in the blessings of community created in the name of the One who suffered on behalf of all.—Doctrine and Covenants 161:3a

Scriptural Expectations

As with many things, today's encounter with an idea has its roots in experiences of times past. Thinking through Christian hospitality issues is one idea that has powerful connections with the ancient world. God was often portrayed in scripture as a gracious and generous host. Quail and manna were provided daily for a hungry and often ungrateful people. Living water was offered in a dry and hot land. Israel's covenant identity included being a stranger, alien, and tenant in God's land. Jesus welcomed children, prostitutes, tax collectors, soldiers, and sinners into his presence. In early Hebrew and Christian thought, the manner in which people treated other people—especially strangers and outsiders—signaled the manner in which they treated God.

The Old and New Testaments both regard hospitality as an obligation. The biblical texts do not question the worthiness of the needy stranger but instead examine the faithfulness of the one from whom hospitality is needed. People throughout the Mediterranean world regarded the provision of food, lodging, and protection as a virtue and sacred duty. All guests were seen as potential friends. Obviously, the stranger can represent a friend or an enemy, but the starting assumption in the ancient Near East was that the stranger was a potential friend. Names were not exchanged until after the meal was eaten, if at all. An exchange of names and background information was not considered a requirement for hospitality.[7]

Scripture Focus—Abraham and Sarah —Genesis 18:1–14

[1] The Lord appeared to Abraham by the oaks of Mamre, as
he sat at the entrance of his tent in the heat of the day. [2]He
looked up and saw three men standing near him. When he
saw them, he ran from the tent entrance to meet them, and
bowed down to the ground. [3]He said, "My lord, if I find favor
with you, do not pass by your servant. [4]Let a little water be
brought, and wash your feet, and rest yourselves under the
tree. [5]Let me bring a little bread, that you may refresh your-
selves, and after that you may pass on—since you have come
to your servant." So they said, "Do as you have said." [6]And
Abraham hastened into the tent to Sarah, and said, "Make
ready quickly three measures of choice flour, knead it, and
make cakes." [7]Abraham ran to the herd, and took a calf, ten-
der and good, and gave it to the servant, who hastened to

prepare it. [8]Then he took curds and milk and the calf that he
had prepared, and set it before them; and he stood by them
under the tree while they ate.
[9]They said to him, "Where is your wife Sarah?" And he said,
"There, in the tent." [10]Then one said, "I will surely return to you
in due season, and your wife Sarah shall have a son." And Sar-
ah was listening at the tent entrance behind him. [11]Now Abra-
ham and Sarah were old, advanced in age; it had ceased to be
with Sarah after the manner of women. [12]So Sarah laughed to
herself, saying, "After I have grown old, and my husband is old,
shall I have pleasure?" [13]The LORD said to Abraham, "Why did
Sarah laugh, and say, 'Shall I indeed bear a child, now that I am
old?' [14] Is anything too wonderful for the LORD? At the set time I
will return to you, in due season, and Sarah shall have a son."

In Genesis 18:1–14, Abraham offered hospitality to three strangers without being aware of the divine nature of the strangers. Abraham and Sarah's hospitality was consistent with the practice in the ancient Near East and included the following elements: Abraham bowed to the strangers; he offered them water, rest, and food; they accepted; the meal was prepared and included a calf, which would have been reserved for a special occasion, and butter, which was greatly prized by the nomad; Abraham waited on his guests while they ate; the strangers did not reveal their identity or offer any gift or payment before the meal.[8]

In sharing the calf and the butter, Abraham and Sarah gave far more than custom required. They chose to treat the three visitors as honored guests, and they did so without expecting anything in return. In verses 9–14, one of them told Sarah that she would have a son. The fact that the gift of a child was promised can be seen as a response to their hospitality; but the promise of a son had already been made in the preceding chapter. The hospitality existed for its own sake, and Abraham has been lifted up as a model because of it.

Reflection

Had Abraham and Sarah refused hospitality to the strangers, they would have shut themselves off from the blessings that God intended—not just the blessing of a son, but also the blessing of God's presence.

- When have you been welcomed by someone who was a stranger? What were the blessings of that encounter?
- In what ways have you experienced God's presence through someone's welcome?

Offering Shelter and Protection

Not only does the New Testament portray Jesus as a gracious host, but Jesus is also portrayed as a vulnerable guest and needy stranger. He is one who "came to his own home" and often received no welcome (John 1:11). "In his life on earth, Jesus experienced the vulnerability of the homeless infant, the child refugee, the adult with no place to lay his head, the despised convict."[9] Throughout his life, Jesus depended on strangers for food and shelter.

A study of the history of the church reveals that hospitality was understood to encompass the physical, social, and spiritual dimensions of human existence and relationships. It meant responding to the physical needs of strangers, offering food, shelter, and protection. But hospitality also included the recognition of the stranger's worth and common humanity. In ancient times, hospitality included protection of the guest and, when extended by a particular household, the entire community was also bound to protect that guest.[10]

When most of the ancient hospitality traditions were being shaped, every stranger was dependent on someone else's hospitality. In the ancient world, there was not the luxury of a drug store, service station, or clinic every few miles. And dependence on personal hospitality had little to do with lack of resources. Strangers were not necessarily destitute, only away from home and in immediate need of food and shelter. Providing hospitality to them was the customary practice.

Today in the developed world, many of us have resources. We can usually avoid depending on the personal hospitality of strangers for the basic resources of food, shelter, and safety We have become accustomed to being able to take care of our own needs. Most people do not want to be seen as "needy." So those of us fortunate enough to be able to meet our own basic needs often find ourselves separated from others who have specific needs.

Unless we travel in a foreign country, live through the devastation of a storm or an earthquake, or run into car trouble on the road, we're unlikely to know what it is to be a vulnerable stranger needing someone else's help. In a highly individualistic and commercial society, depending on the generosity of others is difficult and sometimes feels degrading. Whereas in ancient times all strangers depended on someone else's hospitality, today, it is those without resources who depend most on the free provision of food, shelter, and protection that characterizes hospitality.[11]

The Importance of Food and Fellowship

Biblical hospitality is an act of worship, particularly the act of eating together. As we sit down and share life, we share ourselves. We bond in new ways, experiencing the Christ in one another. Our food becomes more than food when we share it as Christians. It becomes an event of grace—a transforming event.

Food in the ancient world held a sacred meaning that is almost lost in North America, yet even for us there is that sense that eating together implies a deeper relationship. We don't feel comfortable eating in front of just anybody.... We intuitively know that eating together lets down your guard. In ancient traditions...the act of eating together can turn enemies into friends.[12]

Sharing food is an important part of hospitality. In every culture, hardly ever is one invited in without the offer of at least something to drink. Food and fellowship go together. You can be hospitable without offering food right away, but the guests who walk in our doors will eventually need nourishment.

A basic characteristic of hospitality is enabling the guest to feel celebrated. The host makes the others feel that their lives are interesting, worthy of a feast. It doesn't just happen in our homes. Every major event in our lives involves food. Weddings, graduations, and retirements have receptions, funerals have dinners, baby showers have party snacks, and birthdays have cakes. Churches have potluck dinners.

As with other Christian practices, Jesus is our model for fellowship with food. What is remarkable in the Gospels is not the fact that Jesus eats and drinks, but that so much attention is given to reporting that he does. Whether in the simple act of breaking bread or the details of a banquet or wedding feast, Jesus' meals seem to deserve special mention. For the Gospels, meals with Jesus are momentous events, worthy of comment and remembrance. Who he is, is revealed in the meals he shares. He graces the meal he attends. What matters is not his presence but his activity. Jesus always gives more than he receives.[13]

Hospitality, because it was such a fundamental human practice, always included family, friends, and influential contacts. The distinctive Christian contribution was the emphasis on including the poor and needy, the ones who could not return the favor. This focus did not diminish the value of hospitality to family and friends; rather, it broadened the practice so that the close relations formed by table fellowship and conversation could be extended to the most vulnerable.[14]

Around a table, family and guest share food and life. Providing a meal for guests does not need to involve elaborate menus any more than welcoming them requires well-furnished guest rooms or an elegant house. We honor guests as we focus our primary attention on them, not on the food that is served. In our congregations, we need to pay attention to our guests, ensuring that the food we offer benefits both the body and the spirit.

Sharing Our Resources

Avoiding the demands of hospitality is fairly easy today. In fact, hospitality could be considered a lost art in our fast-paced, isolated world. Many Christians have difficulty practicing hospitality not because their cupboards are bare of food and drink, but because they don't take the time. It seems our lives are too full to make room for strangers. We may rationalize, "I'd like to be with you, but I have to work, pick up the children, run to the store, and mow the lawn before dark. There's just not time." The good host takes time, and the effort is noticed and cherished.

> **Why spend precious time making a soufflé when tuna sandwiches will serve the same purpose!... You can say the same thing about homemade valentines, handwritten letters, and handmade quilts. They are frivolous, time-consuming, and inefficient things...their very frivolity and pointless effort speak volumes about the feelings we have for the people we give them to. Sometimes love must be expressed in extravagance, in foolishness, in wild abandon!**[15]

Because God gives and loves graciously, God calls us as disciples of Jesus Christ to be generous in all our relationships and commitments. We encounter Jesus' generous nature through scripture stories. Through them we learn that generosity is rooted not just in giving, but also in receiving.

A disciple practices generosity as a spiritual discipline in response to God's grace and love. "Our hearts are stirred when we realize what we have received from God. We, in turn, want to share...we practice generosity as a spiritual discipline of receiving and giving."[16] [*Becoming a Generous Disciple: Six Principles to Live By*, (Independence, Missouri: Community of Christ, 2004), 5.] Jesus made repeated references to the appropriate use of our earthy possessions. His words and actions help us understand that how we use our resources is an important way for us to be instruments of God's grace and love. We learn to exercise our generosity one decision at a time. As a spiritual discipline, generosity develops as it is exercised.

Interestingly, many ideas, goals, or attitudes become more real, defined, and meaningful when they cost us something. This is also true for hospitality. We should consider how hospitality and money are connected, and how hospitality relates to the call to be generous stewards.

Money has the potential to outlive us. When we provide hospitality, we spend money on things—usually food and housing. The resources we buy and use to be welcoming are often gone by the time the visit is over. However, the honor and love those purchases represent can endure. In fact they have the potential to last forever. The relationships, the miracles that happen as a result of hospitality, can have a lasting effect. "Money's circle of influence can be greater than ours. Many times we give such simple gifts, gifts that cost us very little. But when we give them in the name of Jesus, something happens. God takes our small gifts and multiplies their worth."[17]

Money and the possessions we buy with money are shallow imitations of the riches God can give us. When we use our money in ways that honor God, our small physical offerings can be used to help bring salvation and blessing. It serves as a way of returning a portion of God's blessings. When we share resources with others, it is a stewardship of gratitude.

> **Through receiving God's love and grace, we are liberated to share them. Our ability to give and be generous emerges from a spirit of thankfulness and not obligation. When we extend our lives in service to others, we learn that we receive even as we are giving. Giving and receiving integrate in a circular relationship where one prompts the other. We receive God's gifts. We share them with others. Our giving blesses us and opens up an opportunity for new relationships. And the cycle continues.**[18]

Sharing Our Story
Paul Snethen—Des Moines, Iowa

In the fall of 2005, an e-mail was broadcast to the Des Moines area pastors seeking housing for a doctor for a few weeks as she went through some specialized training for heart-related surgery.

I forwarded the request on to my congregation and went on with life. As I looked over e-mails to delete, something drew me to this request from the pastor of the Clear Lake congregation and prompted me to talk with my wife, Linda, about offering our home. We replied to the pastor and our offer was quickly accepted. Arrangements were made for Dr. Lee to come stay with us a few days a week for about six weeks.

Our guest worked long hours, and we would occasionally visit with her in the late evening if she arrived before our bedtime. She would drive from the Clear Lake area on Monday, work all day, and arrive at our home around 9:00 p.m., or sometimes later. Thursday evenings, we would visit with her, knowing she wouldn't be back until the following Monday because she would drive to her home in Clear Lake on Friday afternoon or evening to spend time with her children over the weekend. On Monday, she would be back.

The short time we had with Dr. Lee was pleasant and interesting as we visited about her work. When she finished and left for the last time, we were showered with gifts that included a large bag of rice and a check for our accommodations. We were surprised by the generosity and questioned accepting the gifts. We were assured that the money and gifts were appropriate, and our guest was emphatic that she preferred our home over a motel room. She indicated that she might need to come back for additional training and would contact us when she knew that was to happen.

Practical Helps for Congregations

Consider the following suggestions. Make note of one or two that your congregation can work to implement in the coming weeks.

In the family (loving your own people):

- Provide "Way to Go!" notes to volunteers and leaders.
- Once a month acknowledge birthdays and anniversaries.
- Phone people on their birthdays.
- Provide care packages to college students and military service personnel who are away from home.
- Deliver a special gift/note for married couples on their wedding day.
- Remember a special gift/note to welcome newborn babies.

Be intentional about saying hello and good-bye:

- Within two minutes of the beginning of a service, visitors have formed an opinion about whether the congregation is friendly. Be ready to make a great impression early on.

- Station greeters at all entrances, in classroom areas, around the sanctuary, and in the parking lot or entry walks.
- Identify your greeters and ushers with a special badge or name tag so visitors who need information can easily identify them.
- Encourage friendly, outgoing people with the gift of "hospitality" to serve as greeters and ushers. Don't expect that just anyone can do these jobs well. Provide regular training that helps them see the church through a visitor's eyes.
- Escort newcomers to the nursery, classrooms, coffee hour, and so on. Don't just point the way or give directions. Go the extra mile to assist.
- Adopt the three-minute rule, which says that members will not talk to other members in the first three minutes following the service. Three minutes is typically how long it takes a guest to exit.
- If you aren't sure if the person you are greeting is a member or a guest, say, "I'm not sure we've met before..."
- Ask outgoing church members to sit in the locations where visitors most commonly sit, often near the entrance or in the back.
- Station someone at every exit to shake hands and thank people for coming. Worship participants can do this since their faces will be familiar.

Help guests feel at home in worship:

- Accept and encourage casual attire.
- Do not ask visitors to stand and identify themselves. Seventy percent of new attendees feel negatively about being recognized. However, they do expect people to be friendly and welcoming.
- Review your church bulletin and other printed material to make sure information is not insider oriented. Avoid church jargon and assuming that people understand the context.

- Make sure the order of worship is easy to read and easy for a visitor to follow. Include written and verbal explanations of what is going on and why. Provide the words to all prayers, songs, and responses that the congregation will participate in.
- Sing at least one hymn each Sunday that is well known outside the church.
- Include a welcome to visitors in the opening words before the service. Make sure the person speaking identifies him or herself.
- Remember that visitors often arrive a few minutes late. Don't frontload in your welcoming comments all the information directed at them.
- Place information about your church's ministries where a guest can easily find it—preferably in the pew or a clearly marked location near the entry points used by visitor. Don't expect guests to go someplace else to find it.
- Prepare guest packets to be handed out by greeters with information about your church programs.
- As they enter worship, give guests with small children a small activity packet with soft, quiet activities.
- Avoid talk about money and budgets with visitors.
- Keep the discussion of "family business" to a minimum in the services. Limit announcements.

Care for children in worship:

- Greet the children who sit near you.
- Express your joy in having children as part of the worshiping community.
- Be sure to smile at the children.
- Help children follow the order of worship or find pages in the hymnal or Bible.
- Pass the offering plate to the children, not over their heads or around them.

- Occasionally invite a child to sit with you during worship.
- Answer a child's question. It is less disruptive to whisper an answer than to shush a child.

Follow up with visitors:

- Get the names and addresses of first-time guests. Some churches use visitor cards, but asking all worshipers to record attendance makes it more likely visitors will sign. Visitors don't want to be singled out.
- Make a special effort to remember the names of guests and call them by name.
- Make at least one follow-up contact with first-time guests within 24 to 36 hours after their visit. It is best to offer a personal, face-to-face or voice-to-voice contact. However, a follow-up letter from the pastor, a phone call, a handwritten note, or an e-mail message is an option to consider. Many churches deliver a gift, such as freshly baked bread, cookies, or a coffee mug, to visitors' homes.
- Develop a system or database for keeping track of guests, their contact information, and the frequency of the visits. A mailing list of past visitors is one of your best marketing tools.
- Don't overlook visitors who come to the church for the first time for an event other than worship. Children's activities, such as summer camps or vacation Bible school, are often great connection points with guests.
- Once someone has attended three times, they should be invited to join the church with a pastoral visit and/or an invitation to participate in an inquirer's or new-member class.
- Encourage guests to get connected with activities and groups, even if they are not ready to join.

Chapter 3

Recognizing the Stranger, Remembering the Guest

> Be patient with one another, for creating sacred community is arduous and even painful. But it is to loving community such as this that each is called. Be courageous and visionary, believing in the power of just a few vibrant witnesses to transform the world.
>
> —Doctrine and Covenants 161:3c

Scripture Focus—The Good Samaritan —Luke 10: 29–37

29 But wanting to justify himself, he asked Jesus, "And who
is my neighbor?" 30 Jesus replied, "A man was going down from
Jerusalem to Jericho, and fell into the hands of robbers, who
stripped him, beat him, and went away, leaving him half dead.
31 Now by chance a priest was going down that road; and when
he saw him, he passed by on the other side. 32 So likewise a
Levite, when he came to the place and saw him, passed by on
the other side. 33 But a Samaritan while traveling came near
him; and when he saw him, he was moved with pity. 34 He went

to him and bandaged his wounds, having poured oil and wine on them. Then he put him on his own animal, brought him to an inn, and took care of him. [35]The next day he took out two denarii, gave them to the innkeeper, and said, 'Take care of him; and when I come back, I will repay you whatever more you spend.' [36]Which of these three, do you think, was a neighbor to the man who fell into the hands of the robbers?" [37]He said, "The one who showed him mercy." Jesus said to him, "Go and do likewise."

When it comes to extending a welcome or a helping hand to a stranger or someone in need, many of us are not free of the critique we place on people in need. Problematic in the helping model is the concern many have about determining who is deserving of hospitality. Early Christian preachers speak of this phenomenon over and over. When a stranger knocks on the door, or when the sick seek aid, Christians often go through extensive mental calculations to determine whether this person is a worthwhile investment, whether the needs are legitimate, whether he or she will use the resources offered wisely. Fear of fraud can easily override the impulse to hospitality. This sort of risk assessment and outcome-based decision-making misses the mark of hospitality. It keeps the focus on worthiness rather than on simple presence, or being with.[19]

In the familiar parable of the Good Samaritan, found in Luke 10:25–37, nothing is said about the worthiness of the person who was injured. No questions were raised about whether or not he might have started the conflict or might have been drunk or on drugs or merely "had it coming." The behavior of the one in need was not being evaluated. The priest, the Levite, and the Samaritan were the ones whose behavior was evaluated—and only one of the three had acted in an acceptable way according to biblical standards. The starting point for the Samaritan was one of acceptance and compassion.

Reflection

- When have you taken time from the busyness of life to share with a neighbor or stranger in need?
- In what ways have the activities of a busy life diverted your attention away from providing ministry?
- When has someone taken time from a hectic schedule to focus on one of your needs?
- When have you been "passed by" or "left hanging" due to someone's busyness or hectic schedule?

The Power of Recognition

When we label someone a stranger, it is usually because that person is unknown or represents something different or unknown to us. If we think about it, we each are strangers, too. Even though we may be blessed with a multitude of resources and are surrounded by close connections through friends and family, there are many people in the world who don't know who we are and who don't know anything about us. As unlikely as it may sound to label ourselves, we must remember that to many people we are strangers.

However, strangers are not only people who are unknown to us; many times they are also those who are disconnected from basic relationships that give people a secure place in the world. They are often detached from family, community, church, and work. People without a place who are also without financial resources are sometimes the most vulnerable people. They not only lack supportive connections with other human beings, but they also are unable to purchase many of the basic necessities of life.

If we look closely at the specific categories of people who warrant hospitality in biblical texts, we will see that they have one thing in common: they are all vulnerable populations. They exist on the margins, both socially and economically. They can easily be ignored and seldom bring status or financial gain to those who reach out to them. Many individuals who are not valued by the larger community are essentially invisible to it. When people are socially invisible, their needs and concerns are not acknowledged and no one even notices the injustices they suffer. Offering hospitality can begin a journey toward visibility and respect. When we offer hospitality to strangers, we welcome them into a place to which we are somehow connected—a place that has meaning and value to us.

When hospitality is offered, the stranger is welcomed into a safe, personal, and comfortable place, a place of respect, acceptance, and friendship. Even if only briefly, the stranger becomes the guest and is included in a life-giving and life-sustaining network of relations. Such welcome involves attentive listening and a mutual sharing of lives and stories. It requires an open heart, a willingness to make one's life visible, and a generosity of time and resources.

Sometimes hospitality can be viewed as quaint or, in some respects, tame. This is partly because we do not understand the power of recognition. When a person who is not valued by society as a human being with dignity and worth is received by a socially respected person or group, small transformations begin to occur. The person's self-assessment, so often tied to society's assessment, is enhanced. This welcoming of the stranger often cuts across the accepted grain of our ordered society. But because such actions are countercultural, they are a witness to the larger community, which is then challenged to reassess its standards and values. When this happens we are witnesses to God's kingdom among us. It is a bit like recognizing a part of God in the stranger. Seeing Jesus in every guest reduces our inclination to try to calculate the importance of one guest over another. If we get to the point of behaving as if every person deserves the most gracious and generous welcome possible, our discipleship reflects more closely the image of the Christ.

Sharing Our Story
Sergio Juarez—La Nueva Esperanza en Cristo, Los Angeles, California

One evening around 7:00 p.m., some members of La Nueva Esperanza en Cristo Congregation were getting ready to go to our Tuesday Bible study, when one of them noticed that someone was sitting on the ground about twenty feet from where we were. He went to check on this person and saw him crying. It was a young man in his early twenties.

When he asked him what the problem was, the young man answered, "I am sick. I had an accident and fell from the second floor and landed on my head, breaking my skull, and some part of my brain was removed along with some bone from my skull. I was sent home after four months in the hospital, and this was my home," he said, pointing to the house behind him. "I came but the landlord told me that I can't go inside now because I didn't pay my rent. I told him that I was in the hospital unconscious and forgot where I lived until yesterday. The landlord sold all my belongings including my clothing," he said crying. "I do not know what to do or where to go. I have no money, because the owner of the factory denies the accident happened at work. The owner says I am not one of his workers so I can't get any benefit now until my attorney wins."

The members of our congregation came to me and said, "Pastor, this man is Jesus; remember what he said, 'Every time you feed, clothe, and give shelter to the needy you are doing it to me.' "

I said, "Yes, this is a great opportunity to do something for someone in need. Let's feed him, clothe him, and give him shelter until he can go somewhere else."

We informed our mission center leadership of this situation, and they added their support to our efforts. We brought the man to the church building and let him stay in the room that we used for classes.

Soon after, his family came to take care of him and took him to another place. He is now doing well, and pretty soon he is going to have surgery to replace the piece of skull that he is missing. He is thankful to the Community of Christ, and he and his family come to visit us in our services.

It would have been easy to close our eyes to this man and to have gone on to our Bible class, but we chose to have our Bible class lived out in a practical way instead of just a theoretical one. Our congregation has learned a lot from this experience and has become exited about what we can do. Now this person, who was once a stranger in need, tells others about our loving care for him. Others have come to see what it is that makes the Community of Christ extend kindness to a stranger. When they ask us we say, "Jesus said, 'If you love me, keep my commandments; and love your neighbor as you would love yourself.' It is simple love in action."

Scripture Focus—Mary and Martha —Luke 10: 38–42

38Now as they went on their way, he entered a certain vil-
lage, where a woman named Martha welcomed him into her
home. 39She had a sister named Mary, who sat at the Lord's feet
and listened to what he was saying. 40But Martha was distract-
ed by her many tasks; so she came to him and asked, "Lord,

do you not care that my sister has left me to do all the work by myself? Tell her then to help me." 41 But the Lord answered her, "Martha, Martha, you are worried and distracted by many things; 42 there is need of only one thing. Mary has chosen the better part, which will not be taken away from her."

Reflection

- With which sister's role do you most often identify? Why?
- If you're a Martha type, how might you become more like Mary—to be more present in the situation?
- Since Martha's role is also important, if you're a Mary type, what can you learn from Martha's devotion to her tasks?
- How can a person balance between the being and doing aspects of hospitality?

The story of sisters Mary and Martha, found in Luke 10:38–42, offers the reader several principles related to hospitality. Martha thought she understood not only the value, but also the concept of true hospitality. That concept included a tasty meal and having the house just right. Like many of us, she spent her time working toward this perfection. The details of the task all seemed to call for her attention at the same time. Her guests had real physical needs and what she offered was necessary work, important work. To neglect any stranger was to breach the moral code.

As Martha scurried about, her sister Mary was sitting at the feet of Jesus, of all things! Mary knew hospitality was of great importance. Martha was angry—even at Jesus: "Lord, do you not care that my sister has left me to do all the work by myself?" (Luke 10:40). The question was really an accusation. How could Jesus, knowing the significance of the task at hand, allow Mary to neglect her duty? Martha felt betrayed. Ironically, when she expressed her anger, her complaint turned into self-indictment. Jesus turned to her and said, "Martha, Martha, you are worried and distracted by many things; there is need of only one thing. Mary has chosen the better part, which will not be taken away from her" (Luke 10:41–42). His words carried no harshness, yet there was the sting of disappointment. Martha was so concerned about the kind of hospitality she wanted to provide that she became inhospitable. In her grand moment of welcoming, she became a barrier to that welcome. She was so anxious and troubled, so caught up with the entanglements of life, that she did the unthinkable thing. She forgot the guest.[20]

Mary and Martha's experience provides a starting point for a definition and practice of biblical hospitality. The story illuminates four key principles of hospitality. These principles are highlighted here, but can be found in full detail in Michele Hershberger's book, *A Christian View of Hospitality*, pages 24–30.[21]

1. **We must first experience God's hospitality**. Many scholars have used this story as an illustration of the dichotomy between contemplation and the active life. For Luke, service is highly valued, but if it is grounded in anything other than a transformative experience with God, it is unacceptable. True listening to God leads to acts of mercy, justice, and kindness—acts of hospitality....Together Mary and Martha represent the proper response of hospitality. Both the doing and the being...are important. As they are balanced...these make for the hospitable place and attitude.

2. **Our hospitality must allow for the fluidity of the host and guest roles**. For Mary, hospitality was not so much offering a service as it was receiving a gift. Martha failed to see that the real host was the one who came as a guest....In true hospitality, the guest many times becomes the host....The

roles blend and merge, gifts are exchanged, and the Divine is present.

3. True hospitality changes the status quo. Rabbis did not allow women to sit at their feet...to be disciples, let alone listen to the lesson. It was one thing for Mary to be at the feet of Jesus...but to be listening, to be drinking in his words, presented a major shift from the status quo. Jesus completed the cultural turnaround when he praised Mary's decision over Martha's. Martha was doing the expected thing...designated to her by her society. Mary, on the other hand, was finding her identity in a role forbidden to her. Jesus, functioning as host, offered Mary a wildly liberating option. In his hospitality, he opened the door for new possibilities—a new way of looking at the world....When we practice true hospitality, our personal status quo gets changed too. That new way of looking at the world comes to the host as well as to the guest. When we see the stranger in a new way, when we think of ministry with someone instead of to someone, our values are questioned, our views are broadened...

4. True hospitality pays attention to the guest. Paying attention to the guest is essential. Jesus was teaching Martha, and us as well, that hospitality to the preacher could not be separated from hospitality to the message. The hospitality that pays attention to the guest is the hospitality that receives the guest unconditionally, that listens to hear the word of the Master through the guest.

Both the "being" and "doing" of hospitality are important. Allowing ourselves to be caught up in only one side of this relationship can be problematic for all. As hosts, if we separate ourselves from our guests by becoming immersed in temporal tasks, we most likely will not experience any form of true togetherness with others. We miss the blessing that hospitality offers to our relationship.

Exploring the Role of Host

Just as we must ask who the stranger is, we must also ask who the host is. On the face of it, we might think of the host as the moral agent, the one who acts for, or on behalf of, the other. There is no doubt that hosts have resources, whether it is food, shelter, or connections. By definition, a host makes those resources available to the stranger/guest. However, the host also receives by participating in hospitality.

The host can receive because the guest does not always come empty handed. Often, guests are the ones with special gifts or insights to share. Through the association, each is blessed. "Biblical stories help us to realize not just that hospitality is an important virtue, but even more that in the context of hospitality guest and host can reveal their most precious gifts and bring new life to each other."[22]

Reciprocity between host and guest is a common occurrence in acts of hospitality. Often those we welcome, welcome us in return. Our guests become our hosts and we, as hosts, become the guests. We would be wrong to only think of ourselves as hosts to our guests who come to church. When we open our eyes to what the stranger can offer us, we can allow ourselves room to receive the guest and the gift. Getting to this point is important, but it is often a difficult step. In it we allow ourselves to become vulnerable and open to other people and what they have to offer us.

> **It is common for us to identify almost automatically with the host, but seldom with the stranger. This may be partly due to belief that the position of host carries greater power. But it may also be due to the greater clarity often given to the host's**

identity...the host is frequently identified by name or position, and so, has a concrete identity. The "other" is faceless and nameless, merely the unidentified stranger or the sick. It is easy to fall into the pattern of thinking that "we" are the hosts and "they" are the guests.[23]

The idea of mutual mission has entered church vocabulary in the last several decades, but it is still difficult to let this concept into our hearts. Some of us feel we need to be self-sufficient and don't want to let anyone know we are in need. Perhaps we do not see how someone with less wealth, or social standing, or education, or faith, or any number of fewer things could provide anything we might need. However, many have testified that when reaching out to someone with a special need, they were given the greater gift just by offering the gift of hospitality to begin with. What we give often comes back in unexpected ways.

An important transformation occurs when people without power or status have the opportunity to be more than guests, when they, too, can be hosts. It is a time when their contributions can be recognized and when they are not defined first by their need. One example is the story of Jesus' visit to Zacchaeus's home, found in Luke 19:1–10. Jesus is first received as a guest and then later transitions into the host in the tax collector's own home.

Combining care with respect—recognizing dignity and seeing the person's need—is a distinctive feature of Jesus' ministry. Instead of disregarding and dishonoring the least among the crowd, Jesus recognized the worth of each. Recognition involves accepting the dignity and equal worth of all people and valuing their contributions, or their potential for contributing, to the larger society. This intermingling of guest and host roles in the person of Jesus is part of what makes hospitality so compelling for Christians. Jesus welcomes and also needs welcome. Likewise, Jesus requires that followers depend on and provide hospitality.

The role of host is empowering because it is an acknowledgment that one has rightful access to a place of meaning and value, and that one has the authority to welcome others into it. The host role affirms that what we have and what we offer are valuable. A large part of what disciples have to offer is welcome into the fellowship found within the body of Christ.

Offering Our Best: The Difference between Trick or Treat, Thanksgiving Feast, and Opening Our Own Refrigerators

Disciples may be surprised at the answers they'd get if they honestly asked, "What would our evangelism look like if we considered a stranger—someone not like us, someone who did not believe like us, someone whose life was very different than ours, someone whose opinions were strange to us, someone whose appearance or language or economic status was foreign to us—as a guest of Christ? Or even as Christ himself? What would our evangelism look like if we saw our role as that of host?" These questions strike at the center of the hospitality issue. "If, when we open the door, we are oriented toward seeing Jesus in the guest, then we welcome that person with some sense that God is already at work in his or her life. This can fundamentally change our perspective and our sense of the dimensions of the relationship. We are more sensitive to what the guest is bringing to us, to what God might be saying or doing through her or him."[24]

In a sense, how we view our homes correlates with our attitudes toward strangers. Do we see our home as a castle with a moat around it and towers from which we can defend our property and those who live there? Do we see our home as a gathering place? Do we like to entertain? Do we see our home as a get-away or an escape from the pressures of life? Do we want to avoid bringing problems or controversy into the home? Do we see our home as a continuing project or work of art? Do we take great pride in the design, the furnishing, and the cleanliness of our home? Do we find ourselves feeling resentful when other people are in our home, or do we covet opportunities to welcome people? Is our home like a busy train station with lots of people passing through all the time—some of whom we know well and some not at all well? The keys to one's images of home are the relationships that currently are present or that have been found there in the past. These relationships are important and often have lasting impact.

We know that when we welcome someone, food is usually a consideration or a part of the welcome. We also know that what is offered and served comes in a variety of styles—each with its own level of formality or intimacy. Sometimes when the stranger/guest comes it's a brief, casual encounter, a little like "trick or treat"—the act of offering a small snack sometimes dictated by polite societal customs. This type of hospitality will most likely be a passing event, not worthy of long-term memory. Yet for the moment, it may be enough.

Other times when the guest arrives, we usher them into an elaborately prepared banquet—a little like a Thanksgiving feast—will all the trimmings and formality that a special occasion offers. During this visit we break out the good dishes, linen, and silverware. This type of hospitality can show respect and value of the guest who is received. It becomes noteworthy to the guest, because of the effort and care extended by the host.

A third type of hospitality is like inviting a guest to raid your home's refrigerator—allowing the guest the status of "being at home" in your home. It says, "You are welcome to everything we have." In this type of hospitality we lay our lives open to our guests. We offer to them our best and our worst. We offer them access to ourselves—who we are and where we live. We give them permission to enter and be part of us. We allow them to sort through the good, bad, fresh, and stale parts of who we are. This level of intimacy will be remembered.

Offering food and drink to one's guests is central to almost every act of hospitality. Next to that, the most important expression of welcome is giving someone our full attention. Even if it is only a brief encounter, giving someone our focused attention communicates welcome. Giving a person our attention requires that we stop and focus on them. This is a challenge today in a society that celebrates the capacity to do several things simultaneously, and in which people seem to take pride in their busyness. However, some things cannot be done quickly. Hospitality takes time. Because it is not a discipline that comes easily to everyone, it is a discipline that must be developed by practice and nurtured with patience.

> **Every contemporary practitioner of hospitality learned the practice from someone else's example—from the "cloud of witnesses" who have gone before, a gracious grandmother, or a wise and generous coworker. People for whom hospitality seems natural are wonderful models from whom to learn the practice. They are living embodiments of welcome; they help us picture what hospitality could look like in our homes, churches, and workplaces. As contemporaries, they help us work out the practical details of an ancient practice.**[25]

If we are to offer our best to our guests, we must offer part of ourselves—our time, energy, skills, talents, resources, listening, our present selves. Because we are unaware of the significance of our friendship and fellowship, sadly, our best resources often remain inaccessible to strangers. We must continually work to recognize the stranger, understand the fluid role of the host, and allow access to our own, authentic lives.

Sharing Our Story—Miami, Oklahoma

Rick serves as pastor of the Miami, Oklahoma, Community of Christ. He met Ernie, founder and director of Freedom from Addiction through Christ (FFATC) through a member of his congregation. FFATC is a rehabilitation facility that ministers to the needs of recovering alcoholic and drug addicts in nearby Picher, Oklahoma. A popular name for this ministry is the "Ark," meaning a safe place to face the storms of life. An invitation was extended to Ernie to visit Miami and share his story and about the work of the Ark with the congregation. A small group attended with Ernie. They shared in story, song, and fellowship, with a potluck meal following the service.

After this initial visit, the Miami congregation invited all the members of the Ark to come to church for a special Sunday service to celebrate Communion followed by continued fellowship at a potluck lunch. Members of the congregation even helped transport members of the Ark community to church.

A few years ago, the Miami congregation was blessed to receive an inheritance. The use of part of these funds was dedicated to community outreach. Each year, the congregation selects a community organization that is significantly benefiting the community and presents a "Spirit of Community" award to recognize and support that group's continued efforts. The first Spirit of Community Award was presented to the FFATC.

The relationship between the two groups has continued, with a transformation of both. When the Ark arrives to worship, members of the Miami congregation are present and in place to greet each person as they enter the building. Coffee, juice, and pastries are waiting in the fellowship hall. Ark members outnumber the congregation and are free to make themselves at home. There are friendly exchanges among everyone as members address friends by name and inquire how things are going. There is a true sense of friendship and family when the groups are together.

On "Ark Sundays" an elaborate potluck lunch is prepared with an abundance of food. The worship services are lively and relevant to the needs of seekers. Special guest ministers, musicians, and puppeteers have been invited to share on those days. Members dress in casual clothing and blue jeans on the days the Ark visits, being sure to eliminate as many barriers as possible so everyone feels welcome. No detail is left to chance—a bucket of sand is placed outside the entrance door to accommodate the needs of those who smoke.

After the meal, members of the Ark all pitch in to clean up the fellowship hall and kitchen. Tables and chairs are put up, the area is vacuumed, and things are returned to their proper places. Watching this activity, one would think this diverse group of ages, races, and experiences were all part of the same extended family.

As the two communities have continued to connect, congregation members have opened their hearts and minds to assist when needs arise. And members of the Ark have come to offer their gifts as well, with some assisting with maintenance projects and music in worship gatherings. Some have even started coming on their own, apart from the regular Ark Sundays.

Association with the Ark has opened doors to ecumenical projects in the community. Members of each group are learning ways to assist the larger community and to further minister to those they encounter. Many lives are affected by addiction, and through FFATC and the Community of Christ, many lives are being touched by the ministry of Jesus Christ.

Currently the Ark is located in Picher, Oklahoma, a depressed area of the state that was heavily mined for decades and is now facing environmental, water, and soil pollution.

The Ark is faced with looking to relocate their ministry. The bond between the two groups is strong, and every effort will be made to maintain the connection in the future.

Practical Helps for Congregations

Consider the following suggestions. Make note of one or two that your congregation can work to implement in the coming weeks.

- Hold an Open House Sunday at least once a year.
- Organize a bring-a-friend Sunday at least once a year, and be prepared to receive guests.
- Extend extra hospitality during back-to-school time, Christmas, and Easter, when people are most likely to consider visiting a church.
- Provide training to members on how to invite others to church. Offer a training session on the resource *Vibrant Witness: Who, Me?* to assist members to identify and articulate their personal testimony.
- Start a personal invitation ministry. Three out of four people attend a church for the first time because they were invited. Yet less than half of church members say they have invited someone in the last year.
- Use the resource *Can I Get a Witness!* to start a witnessing support group for those wanting to reach out to their friends and neighbors.
- Print special invitations to Christmas and Easter services that people can deliver to friends.
- Plan special events—concerts, lectures, game nights, sports events—that appeal to those outside the church and that members feel comfortable inviting someone to.
- Have special recognition Sundays for Scout groups, preschool families, or other community groups meeting in your church to encourage them to attend worship. For ex-

ample, offer a teacher appreciation recognition close to the beginning or end of the school year, thanking the teachers for assisting with the congregation's children.

Chapter 4

Glimpses of the Kingdom: Reclaiming Hospitality in the Church

> **Do not be fearful of one another. Respect each life journey, even in its brokenness and uncertainty, for each person has walked alone at times. Be ready to listen and slow to criticize, lest judgments be unrighteous and unredemptive. —Doctrine and Covenants 161:3b**

Scripture Focus—Feeding the Multitude —Matthew 14:13–21

[13][Jesus] withdrew from there in a boat to a deserted place
by himself. But when the crowds heard it, they followed him
on foot from the towns. [14]When he went ashore, he saw a
great crowd; and he had compassion for them and cured their
sick. [15]When it was evening, the disciples came to him and
said, "This is a deserted place, and the hour is now late; send
the crowds away so that they may go into the villages and buy
food for themselves." [16]Jesus said to them, "They need not go
away; you give them something to eat." [17]They replied, "We

have nothing here but five loaves and two fish." [18] And he said, "Bring them here to me." [19]Then he ordered the crowds to sit down on the grass. Taking the five loaves and the two fish, he looked up to heaven, and blessed and broke the loaves, and gave them to the disciples, and the disciples gave them to the crowds. [20]And all ate and were filled; and they took up what was left over of the broken pieces, twelve baskets full. [21] And those who ate were about five thousand men, besides women and children.

In Matthew 14:13–21, we read of the "miraculous" feeding of the multitude. In many ways, this story serves as a model for how disciples are to receive and care for the needs of strangers and guests. "The crowds that followed Jesus included women and children and others 'not counted'—the sick, elderly, handicapped, disabled, all the people in a society that are not making it—and they are always the majority of the people."[26] Yet this needy crowd seems to have had more going for it than one might have originally thought.

> **No woman in her right mind would head into a deserted place with an elderly person or a child or someone who was sick without taking food, drink, diaper changes, the works....So when the women went after Jesus, they took what they had with them. The real answers to their problems were not in the politics or the structures of the existing society, but in the people themselves, found among those who "do not count." The answers, the hope comes from the bottom up. They are the people who have struggled to live, who have barely survived, and Jesus knew that if he could take what the disciples had and share it, then the others would respond by sharing what they had. Some had brought much, some had probably brought nothing, some had only what they deemed necessary for themselves. Yet, in the sharing, the liturgy and worship that Jesus initiated, there**

was more than enough for them and for the rest of the world (symbolized by the twelve baskets of leftovers).[27]

This story of the feeding of the multitude can serve to remind us that often the ones not counted are the ones with hidden wisdom, hidden powers, hidden truth, and hidden hope for the future. The ones who were not counted had the food, the trust to share, the baskets for collecting the leftovers, and the need to stay all day. It seems that the true miracle was found in the sharing that took place among people in their everyday living and giving. Encountering another person's need provides opportunities for sharing. What is the greater miracle—that Jesus multiplies food unnaturally or that the people see, trust, risk, hope, and share with one another? Often our reluctant gift is blessed and given away to those who are in need. The disciples are a model for behavior, for risking and trusting in a new order, a new way of being with one another and together with Jesus.

In feeding the multitudes, Jesus gave the food to the disciples to share. Another miracle in this story is that Jesus empowered the disciples to do the ministry. He taught them that they had more resources within them than they ever thought possible. Jesus chose to work through them.

Jesus also chooses to work through us. He chooses us to share in the glory and in the blessing. He chooses us to be the fortunate ones to see the miracles, to see the impossible become possible, and to toss huge chunks of God's generosity to people because there is a never-ending supply.[28]

Reflection

The story seems to infer that the disciples thought it impossible or at least inconvenient to attempt feeding such a multitude; they also did not seem to share the compassion that Jesus felt for the crowd. Jesus evidently perceived that the disciples had whatever was needed to take care of the crowd's needs.

- What keeps us from sharing the feast of God's love and grace with others—our pessimism, the inconvenience of it, or our lack of vision or compassion?
- Where do we encounter "hungering multitudes" in our day? How do we go about setting a table for them in the Spirit of Christ?
- Jesus evidently perceived that the disciples had whatever was needed to take care of the crowd's needs. What do you think you have that others need and hunger for?

A Lifetime of Hospitality

As our society becomes more compartmentalized and specialized, it seems that all too often people are also alienated and marginalized. Every person has a deep longing to belong. The thirst for identity, recognition, and dignity is powerful within the human psyche. The heart hungers for connection and affirmation. The story of God's interaction with humankind as recorded in scripture suggests that God created us to long to connect with God and to each other. In effect we were created for community. Creating circumstances (conversations, environments, cultures of attitude, events and social occasions, programs and services, lifestyles and discipleship practices) where that sense of connection and worth is fostered and nurtured is the practice of hospitality.

With the ever-shifting nature of contemporary society, it is increasingly difficult for people to make meaningful connections or to form lasting bonds. This leads to often-shallow relationships, and pass-through friendships. It is to address this need that today's churches hold the most promise. In fact, the most receptive people for churches to reach are those in two categories: those in transition and those under tension. The results of experiencing pain or times of change seem to grab people's attention and make them more receptive to the gospel, God's Spirit, and church fellowship. Any time someone experiences major change, whether positive or negative, it seems to create a hunger for spiritual stability.[29] These times present prime opportunities for congregations to offer genuine, caring hospitality.

Offering hospitality over a lifetime encourages disciples to be aware of the shifting cycles of life happening all around us. Sometimes these shifts are gentle, requiring a perceptive eye or ear to notice. Other times the shifts are monumental, announcing their presence in an overpowering blast of recognition. No matter how the change comes to our attention, lives are affected and the chance to minister through acts of welcome and hospitality become real. What are some of these life-cycle events? They are events that happen throughout the course of our living and can be positive and negative, joyful and disruptive, life-giving and destructive. For starters consider some of the normal passages of life: expecting a child; suffering a miscarriage; giving birth; adopting a new family member; moving to a new home; starting a new job; losing a job; losing a home; children starting school; children leaving home; learning to drive; graduation; dating; engagement; marriage; divorce; death of a child, sibling, spouse, mother or father; health crisis; baptism; ordination; retirement; and so on.

This list can go on and on and can be customized for each individual. However, we will discover many similarities and encounter some differences that will shape how hospitality can be extended during these events that change our lives. Our role is to be aware and ready to assist in recognition of important life events.

It would be a serious error to think of "welcoming ministries" as related only to newcomers. People are always in transition. They often need to be re-welcomed as circumstances in life change. We should not take this for granted.

Making Room, Preparing to Receive

There is an integral connection between hospitality and home. This connection is communicated in the common Hispanic expression of welcome, "*Mi casa es su casa*" or, "My house is your house." How we view our homes correlates to an extent with our attitudes toward strangers. Consider the following questions:

- What are the images of home that come to your mind? Consider especially the nature of the relationships that are found there.
- How has having guests in your home changed through the years?
- When was the last time you had a guest in your home?
- What did you do to get ready for his or her coming?
- What activities preceded your guest's arrival?
- What feelings were present before your guest's arrival, during your guest's visit, and when your guest left your home?
- What feelings do you have when you hear the words, "We're going to have company"?

Our homes are often the most personal settings into which we can invite people. For Christians, the possibility of welcoming Jesus into one's home shaped ancient church teachings on home-based hospitality. Today we must connect our homes in fresh ways to how we see our congregations.

Understanding the church as God's household has significant implications for hospitality. More than anywhere else, when we gather at church our practice of hospitality should reflect God's gracious welcome. God is host, yet we also have opportunities to act as hosts who welcome others.

Outsiders form opinions about us completely apart from hearing us declare our faith, knowing our good intentions, or seeing the creed to which we give verbal affirmation. Our actions define us for outsiders. Those who don't claim to be Christians watch to see whether we live in a way that demonstrates God, follows what we say we believe, and most important, honors their search for God. They want to know whether God cares about them, and we're their source material. Sometimes the very people we hope to touch with the love of God may not like what our lives say about what it means to be a Christian. For those of us whose Christian witness is quite public (pastors, teachers, youth leaders), the response we give to an unexpected guest is connected to how that person experiences God's love and welcome.

Taking time to prepare ourselves and our congregations for guests requires that we first expect to have guests. We may be part of a congregation where guests are a regular occurrence. That's terrific! But what if we're part of a congregation who hasn't seen a guest in a long time? Perhaps part of the reason for that is that we don't expect to have any guests. If that is our mindset, we are already a bit behind. We must take the steps to invite, expect, and prepare for guests.

Consider the notion of hosting a dinner for a few friends at your home. What are the steps you as host take to make this happen? Here are a few of the basic steps undertaken before nearly every visit. As you read this list, think about applying similar actions to our congregational hosting ministries.

- First, an invitation is extended and accepted; a time, date, and location are established.
- Next, a menu is selected with consideration of the guest's interests and of course, with the host's abilities and limita-

tions. (We all are not equipped to be gourmet chefs, and we must each work within our budgets.)

- Needed food and supplies are gathered.
- We clean the house, prepare the food, and prepare ourselves.
- We anticipate the guest's arrival by turning on the porch light, opening the door, watching at the door or window—ready to greet the guest and welcome them in.
- When the guest arrives, we offer to take their coat, offer a tour of the house, show the guest where to sit, offer a drink or snack, and engage in conversation. Usually this conversation is focused on the guest. We ask about how they are, what's going on in their lives, how their work is going, and so on.
- The meal is presented and served. Conversation continues.
- We check to make sure that the guest's needs are satisfied. Do they have what they need? Did they get enough to eat and drink? And so on. All the while, attention is focused on the guest and our time together.
- The visit comes to an end. We thank the guest for coming and escort them to the door. We may walk them out or stand by the door or window to wave good-bye.
- We invite them to come back or we make plans to get together again in the future.

If we consider the elements of this event, almost everything the host did was for the sake of the invited guest. The host's attention was focused on the guest. That is to be expected when we are honored with the guest's visit whether in our homes or congregations.

Similarly to hosting at home, expanding our welcome at church and being a good host takes time. First, we have to simply be there when someone new comes to our church or to our door. Then it takes a relaxed sense of time to nurture relationships. Friendships don't just develop simply by scheduling appointments to get to know people. We experience quality time by investing in quality time. Finally, we speak volumes about how we love someone by how much time we are willing to spend with them. For many of us, time is our most precious resource. When we rush off to meet a deadline, we are communicating what is really important to us.

Attentive leaders recognize that the little things play a key role in the success or failure of any organization. When we invite someone to our homes, we pay close attention to lots of little details. This is also true in the church. First-time visitors often notice the little things. First-time visitors may form a negative impression of the kind of church we are and may never have an opportunity to see our strengths if we have not paid attention to the "little things." For our members, the little things will play an important role in shaping our church's entire culture and how members pursue ministry. Our role is to be aware of how guests experience the ministry we offer and how those little things shape the outcome of those encounters.

> **Every time a first-time visitor walks in the doors of your church an opportunity unfolds. This individual or family has taken the time to worship with you for some reason. Visitors likely have a need they are wondering if you can fulfill. If these persons had their own home churches, they would likely not be visiting, so the chances are that each visitor is one of the non-religious that Jesus came to reach. The question is, What kind of follow-up will you do to encourage each one to come back?**[30]

In the business world, we know that customer service and creating a first impression is vital; so too is extending a proper welcome essential to hospitality and ministry in congregations. An effective greeting ministry can make or break our efforts at sharing our congregation and the "good news" of Christ with visitors. The greeter is often the first person in a restaurant or a church to speak to a guest. First impressions set the tone for everything that follows. During those early seconds, a guest gets a feeling of welcome or indifference, a feeling of being glad she came, or wishing she hadn't. It is important to greet or acknowledge every guest by name whenever possible; use the guest's name aloud immediately and (when convenient) write it down for follow-up; introduce the person to someone else directly or indirectly either before or after the service; when appropriate, ask the guest what he or she does; it's easier to remember a person if you associate him or her with a job or role; don't be afraid to seek out strangers: remember, today's regulars were yesterday's unknowns.[31]

In greeting ministry, it is important to train the greeters. They should know about what happens at the church including classes, events, programs, times, locations, and contact persons. Consistency is important. It may be difficult to remember a guest from the previous week's service if we switch greeters too often. Here are key questions congregations need to consider when developing a greeting ministry:

- Are all doors staffed with greeters?
- Can the greeters be easily identified?
- Do the greeters represent the diversity of the church?
- Are greeters friendly and knowledgeable about what happens at church?
- Is there someone to help young parents know where to go with their children?
- Does your congregation make sure to have someone at the door to greet people leaving after the worship?

Ushers and greeters in welcoming ministries are the most commonly acknowledged roles. One of the simplest ways of communicating welcome is to greet guests at the door or threshold and personally escort them in. Learning guests' names quickly and providing a few introductions can be very reassuring. Guests' arrivals and departures should be specially recognized—an initial welcome and a gracious farewell communicate that their visit was valued. Not everyone can or is willing to assist in this way. However, there are lots of ways people can assist with welcoming/hosting ministries. Here are a few other roles that might benefit the church's welcoming efforts:

- Spotter: Watch for new faces during the service and make a point of talking to these people after worship. Having an exit-greeting strategy is as important as greeting people when they first enter. This ensures that guests are provided with what they need all the way through their visit at the church.
- Feeder: Make sure newcomers get their fill of coffee and other refreshments during hospitality time. Stay attentive to help guests know how to proceed through social experiences that may be complicated to newcomers.
- Tagger: Go out of your way to identify newcomers. Assist with nametags, if they want them, *and only if everyone else is wearing one*, so that guests don't stand out.
- Introducer: Connect new people with others in the congregation. Introduce yourself to the guest *and* introduce the guest to someone else.
- Informer: Stand near the literature racks to answer questions and help people find the information they seek. Be available to assist guests in finding locations in the church.
- Seat-hopper: Sit in a different place in the congregation each week, so you can get to know people in each area.[32]

After a guest comes to church...then what? Our approach to greeting ministry needs to be holistic. It is important to not only greet guests as they arrive, but also be purposeful about their departure and any follow-up ministry that may be needed. Consider these practical suggestions:

- Greet that person again on his or her way out of your church.
- Offer an opportunity to meet with the pastor.
- Invite a guest to lunch or out for coffee.
- Make a follow-up contact with all guests within 48 hours. Send a card, make a call, or drop by with a small gift. Only stay a short time and make the guest feel welcomed to come again.
- Find a way to determine a guest's interests and needs.
- Consider having a fellowship time with refreshments after the service to meet and greet guests.
- When the guest returns, remember that person's name and make a point to connect with that person again.

Learning new skills and being able to view things in a new light are important steps in developing our welcoming and hospitality ministry. Learning to see ourselves in a different light is also crucial to the work of hospitality. We can have all the other elements—seeing the situation differently, seeing the stranger differently, and even seeing God differently, but if we don't assume that God desires to work *through us*, the miracles don't happen. God can empower us for the task. God can take our resources and multiply them. But we also have to believe in ourselves and our abilities. Our faith in God has to apply to us also.[33] Without disciples serving together as the body of Christ, the work won't get done.

Hospitable Worship: Celebrating the Sacraments—Watching Our Language

Worship is often the entry point for visitors and guests to our congregations. Unfortunately, churches have generally done better with offering food programs and providing clothing closets than with welcoming into worship people significantly different from those who regularly attend their congregations.

Welcoming a person to worship and providing for their worship experience is important. For some churches, getting a person to pull in the parking lot and enter the building for the first time is a giant hurdle. Many have intentions of visiting, but find it difficult to make the first step, afraid of what they may encounter. Extending a warm, hospitable welcome takes purposeful planning and a great deal of care. The role of people serving as greeters to welcome guests to God's house is arguably one of the most important roles to fill. Without this welcome, connections are not made, and the likelihood that a first-time guest will return is slim.

Early Christians recognized that hospitality could not be extended to those outside the community if it was not practiced within the community. Attention to hospitality in worship, in dealing with the wayward, in receiving persecuted and exiled Christians, and in resolving internal conflicts, set a tone and an atmosphere that promoted the continuity of hospitality in all aspects of communal life. When these and other details are addressed, many congregations experience growth within their communities.

One primary place where many Christians are rigid and limited in vision deals with how worship is experienced. Like anything, we can find ourselves trapped in a tradition or a practice that once met a particular need, but in many respects may now be meaningless and irrelevant to outsiders. Inviting and welcoming others to come to our congregations is a giant first step to fulfilling the discipleship call. Other steps are necessary for consideration also. We may have clear directions to our church, great signs so visitors find their way, friendly greeters, and powerful programs, but if our worship is not attuned to be visitor friendly and open to others, in many respects we are failing in our outreach and discipleship. Each aspect of church life should be examined regularly. To do so without fear would be a wonderful feat.

Looking at worship through the lens of hospitality should change our perspective. In terms of hospitality, our focus is not simply or even primarily on meeting our own needs. We want to meet the needs of others and especially of those who are strangers to us. If we can remember that the church exists primarily for those who are not yet part of it, then we can better understand our role as the hosts and want the worship service and other elements to be meaningful to our guests.

Congregations that focus on hospitality find a greater acceptance of diversity within existing services of worship, with people recognizing that the needs of others should be met—and especially the needs of those who are guests and who may have had negative past experiences with worship. Congregations that focus on hospitality and have the needed resources in leadership, settings, and membership may create different types of worship opportunities aside from the traditional worship services. Some will offer a contemporary worship service, others a more focused time of prayer and contemplation or small-group devotion. Offering variety in the worship experience serves existing members by letting them select the style that speaks most effectively to them. The variety also serves prospective members, our guests, by giving them the opportunity to experience more than a single style of worship. Unless members of any group make a conscious effort to create programs that will appeal to those outside the group, they naturally default to designing events that reflect their own tastes. Our congregations today must strategically think through how to present the gospel in an environment that will attract those who are in need of it.[34]

Worship should be clear and inclusive. Our worship should be welcoming to all. Our outreach is helped if we are seeker-friendly in worship and other activities. Consider the following helpful suggestions:

- Focus your worship on the good news of the gospel. Show people why you're here.
- Make hospitality a congregational theme.
- To transform lives and the world, we need to be constantly transforming worship.
- Consider your community and local and world events: Is your worship relevant and gospel-filled?
- Use confession: Since no one is perfect, we should avoid coming across as having all the answers.
- Caring and Sharing: Welcome and acknowledge guests without embarrassing them or putting them on the spot.
- Don't presume everyone knows the speaker, pastor, church officials, program emphases, and so on.
- Avoid inside or confusing jokes or announcements.
- Demonstrate concern for kids, youth, the elderly, and the disabled in worship.
- Demonstrate concern for people and programs outside the congregation.
- Help participants connect with the message found in God's word. Provide background (exegesis) on scripture readings. Remember not everyone is a Bible scholar or church historian.
- When celebrating the sacraments, explain each one as if it is being experienced for the first time. Guests are often pres-

ent during these times. It will help them know how they can effectively participate. This also serves to remind members about the importance of these events in their lives.

- Provide opportunity to welcome guests.

Celebrating the sacraments provides prime opportunity for disciples to engage in the ministry of hospitality and welcome. The sacraments are important functions of our worship together. Friends, family, and the community are often encouraged to attend these special life events and share together with the worshiping community. During these occasions, special preparation needs to be made by the congregation to welcome guests, provide information, and witness of Jesus Christ through the sacraments.

Chapter six of the book *The Sacraments: Symbol, Meaning, and Discipleship* offers detailed insight to the topic of invitation and hospitality relating to each of the church's sacraments. A basic premise is that "for all eight sacraments of the Community of Christ to be visitor-friendly instruments of witness and sharing, there must be an attitude and an environment of hospitality."[35] We further honor the intent of the sacraments when we come to see that extending the divine experience found within them means we include others.

Language issues also need to be considered. Every close group has a developed language or way of addressing each other. This is more than just calling each other sister or brother. It involves how we know what to do and what things mean. It is a special knowledge that takes developing. In many ways it signals who is in the "in group." Many of us have lived comfortably in this world long enough that we may have forgotten or perhaps have never experienced what it is like to be outside the "knowing" group.

Nothing makes a person feel more excluded than sitting

in a group where people are having their own private conversation or experience and he or she doesn't have a clue about what is going on! In spoken language, don't presume everyone knows songs, prayers, scriptures, or stories. Avoid or explain in-house jargon or acronyms. Instead, we should intentionally use inclusive language so that others may more readily join in.

In printed messages, people want to know what they're supposed to do. Clear, complete instructions make guests more comfortable and keep them from feeling singled out or unprepared. Consider these helpful suggestions:

- If you use a bulletin, it should extend a prominent welcome to visitors/guests.
- Provide clear instructions to assist worshipers during the service. No steps or responses should be taken for granted. The bulletin should include all the information needed for the service.
- What do HS, SP, and NS, *, +, D&C mean? Visitors should not be expected to be familiar with the church's traditions, shortcuts, or special terminology.
- Why is the offering time called "Disciples' Generous Response"?
- Do guests know who the Communion sacrament is for? Are they allowed to partake? How do you make that clear?
- Make all printed announcement details clear, complete, and concise.
- Use readable print.

Sharing Our Story —Eros, Louisiana

The Eros congregation in Louisiana opened its doors in September 2005 to host evacuees from Lake Charles, Louisiana, during Hurricane Rita. Here is part of that story:

Our hearts were going out to the folks—first, for Hurricane Katrina, and then for Hurricane Rita evacuees. Surprisingly, with that much need, there wasn't much of a coordinated effort for help. We began praying that God would lead us to help the evacuees in ways that were needed. We also began registering and helping the larger community at the Monroe Civic Center shelter as Red Cross volunteers. This proved beneficial, since we obtained a lot of information concerning resources to help and ways to assist.

Our congregational financial officer received a call from the World Church asking if we could help a group of church members from the Lake Charles area. Being able to offer our assistance was like an answered prayer. We said yes, definitely.

The Eros congregation housed the evacuees at the church. We were told there would be about ten or so, so we prepared for twenty. We had seventeen that first day. The highest count of evacuees we housed was fifty. We hosted them for a month.

To assist with the effort, calls went out, and members and friends from the congregation brought supplies—everything that was needed to turn the congregation into an evacuation shelter: food, bedding, water, movies, televisions, games, and so on.

We placed as many families together in classrooms and the nursery as possible. Half of the sanctuary was also made into a sleeping area. Pets were housed outside and bedding and food was provided for them, too.

The Red Cross assisted our efforts by providing food rations and water. They checked in on us every fifth day and were grateful that we had most of the supplies that were needed.

Aside from the day-to-day operations, which included preparing meals and assessing needs, we tried attending to the physical, emotional, and spiritual needs of our guests. Congregation members filled needs as they were assessed. Above all, we tried listening and relating to the evacuees. We understood how devastating a situation they were in, and tried to reassure our guests that we were there for them and would be for as long as it took. We just tried to love them by getting to know them.

We were all together sharing in this devastating time, yet we also had fun times, too. Sometimes the worst thing is to just sit and allow your mind to wander and make room for negative thoughts to enter. So we offered some diversions. Although members and friends had brought TVs, VCRs, DVD players, movies, and games to pass the time, we had a formal movie night complete with popcorn and all sorts of refreshments. And because of a donation by a member of the congregation, some were able to attend the annual fair in Monroe.

We tried making life as bearable as possible for our guests, while relaying information from local and state authorities that would help get their lives back to normal as quickly as possible. All in all, we are thankful that we had the opportunity to get to know these people, our brothers and sisters.

Practical Helps for Congregations

Consider the following suggestions. Make note of one or two that your congregation can work to implement in the coming weeks.

Here are some basic considerations for creation of informational materials.

For congregational newsletters:

- Include good news and upcoming events to invite others to join. Don't just report on past events.
- Provide contact information but protect private information like specific health or prayer needs and personal contact information for members and friends.

- Provide a connection to the larger community. How is your congregation involved with the community around you?
- Who are you as a congregation? What is your focus/mission/vision? What are your strengths?

Text to add to bulletins:

As with all information included in a written announcement, it is vital that all details be considered before publication. Include the details of who, what, when, where, why, and how for each announcement. Examples of additions to bulletins or other publications include:

- Welcome statements suggestions

  1. We are grateful for your presence and invite you to participate in the worship, program, and service life of our congregation.

  2. Welcome! If you've been thinking, praying, searching, and hoping for a place to belong, we've been waiting for you! We believe every person who comes into this fellowship was sent by God. It's not an accident that we have the joy of meeting you now. We wish to express Christ's love to you with warm, genuine caring. We are eager to know you, and are excited to share with you the marvelous ways God is working through our church. It won't take you long to discover that this is a family, rich in relationships that matter. Growing together, we worship, serve, laugh, cry, learn, and reach out to our world to share the peace of Jesus Christ. Our doors and our hearts are open to you.

- Information about Community of Christ beliefs, especially as related to the sacraments during worship. Specific wording can be found in the current informational tracts: Sacraments, Faith and Beliefs, Being a Disciple, Core Values, A

Disciple's Generous Response, Tithing, and World Mission Tithes.

- Information about the nursery and children's and youth classes. Provide details about classroom, nursery, and child care locations and a protection statement. Consider the following:

  Children and Youth Workers Are Registered—The Community of Christ firmly believes in protecting all children and youth who participate in church-sponsored activities. Any adult who provides leadership to children or youth is required to go through an application and training process that necessitates approval before being placed in a leadership position. We are committed to providing a safe, quality, nurturing environment where children and youth are encouraged, loved, and supported.

- A list of adult Christian education classes and inquirers classes that are offered
- An invitation to available Bible study opportunities
- Worship—provide a list of worship opportunities including times and locations. And consider a statement that explains how worship is offered in the Community of Christ. Consider the following examples:

  1. Worship: Ministry through worship is planned and offered by a coordinated effort of ordained ministers and lay participants in our congregational life. Men, women, children, and teens volunteer their time and talents in worship gatherings. Preaching and worship leading comes mostly from ministers who are ordained and trained. This results in a rich variety of worship services and experiences.

  2. Worship gatherings usually include preaching or testimonies, music, prayer, and a special focus for children. On the

first Sunday of each month, our congregation celebrates the Lords' Supper (Communion).

- Disabilities and Special Needs

Everyone, with or without disability, should be welcomed with courtesy and thoughtfulness. Barriers of attitude, communication, and architecture need to be considered. By anticipating the needs of those with disabilities, the atmosphere and conveniences are frequently improved for everyone.

When making announcements about or referring to people with special needs or disabilities, use appropriate terminology and "people-first" language. This refers to the principle that the person is primary and the disability or need is secondary. Our language should affirm rather than diminish individuals. For example, refer to a person as a "worshiper with a disability" rather than a "disabled worshiper." Also, talking about a person who "uses a wheelchair" is better than saying the person is "wheelchair bound" or "confined to a wheelchair." Or a person could say, "The stairs in that building will be a handicap for John, who uses a wheelchair," but not, "John is handicapped and can't use the stairs."[36]

Choose wording in printed bulletin statements with sensitivity. Those with limited mobility will appreciate phrases that allow options. Use "Standing or Seated" or "Kneeling or Seated" instead of phrases like "Congregation Stands" or "Congregation Kneels."[37]

Other things to consider include:

1. Check for adequate lighting and provide large-print bulletins, hymnals, and Bibles to assist those with visual needs.
2. Provide individual listening devices for improved sound quality.
3. Enlist the services of a sign language interpreter for individuals who are deaf.

4. Identify the location of restrooms and child changing stations.
5. Identify the location of elevators, entrance ramps, automatic door openers, and special pathways and parking areas that make it easier for people with disabilities or special mobility needs to enter.

- Instructions to guests

1. Extend an invitation to stay for refreshments when available following class or worship.
2. Announce where and how to learn about the church and its ministries. An inquirers class offers an opportunity to explore church beliefs and membership expectations.
3. When is the church open? List office hours, message machine, Web site, and other contact information.
4. Share information about the congregation's vision and/or mission. For example:

"We are called to 'reach in' to the community of faith at *(specific location and time)* and to 'reach out' beyond the walls of the church with Christ's love and message of hope. We welcome people with diverse gifts and talents to partner with us inputting God's love into action."

5. Provide a statement about involvement and membership opportunities. For example:

"You are invited and welcome at worship, classes, and other gatherings. As you sense the call to become more involved with your ministry, you may wish to formally join with us. For those who feel the call in their life to follow Christ's example and be baptized, we offer this special sacrament for all those eight years of age and older. Membership in the Community of Christ takes place after baptism and confirmation."

- Consider a short list about what's great about being part of the Community of Christ. Use these suggestions or provide your own.

1. We emphasize the worth of each person.
2. We believe in shared ministry among all disciples. Each of us is called to share in fulfilling Christ's mission.
3. We are called to help build community and establish God's peaceable kingdom, which we call Zion.
4. We believe that God continues to speak to us through scripture, giving us ever deeper insight and a sense of personal call.
5. We experience a global fellowship that provides opportunities for worldwide connection and perspectives beyond our own cultural experience.
6. We offer intimate groups of "family" all over the world. In each place, a person can be welcomed like a member of the family.
7. We acknowledge that we understand only a part of what God is doing. We do not have all the answers, but we have opportunity to recognize new facets of God as God continues to reveal new truths and possibilities.
8. We are servants who believe we each are stewards of God's creation, called to preserve and share God's abundant gifts with the world.
9. Our fellowship strives to be open and inclusive. Each disciple is called to participate in the life of the church by sharing gifts, fellowship, testimony, and resources.
10. We place an emphasis on peace, reconciliation, and healing of the spirit.

Chapter 5

We Shall All Be Changed

You hold precious lives in your hands. Be gentle and gracious with one another. A community is no stronger than the weakest within it. Even as the One you follow reached out to those who were rejected and marginalized, so must the community that bears his name.

—Doctrine and Covenants 162:6c

Scripture Focus—Elijah and the Widow —1 Kings 17: 8–16

8 Then the word of the LORD came to him, saying, 9 "Go now
to Zarephath, which belongs to Sidon, and live there; for I have
commanded a widow there to feed you." 10 So he set out and
went to Zarephath. When he came to the gate of the town, a
widow was there gathering sticks; he called to her and said,
"Bring me a little water in a vessel, so that I may drink." 11 As
she was going to bring it, he called to her and said, "Bring me
a morsel of bread in your hand." 12 But she said, "As the LORD
your God lives, I have nothing baked, only a handful of meal
in a jar, and a little oil in a jug; I am now gathering a couple of
sticks, so that I may go home and prepare it for myself and my
son, that we may eat it, and die," 13 Elijah said to her, "Do not
be afraid; go and do as you have said; but first make me a little
cake of it and bring it to me, and afterwards make something

for yourself and your son. [14]For thus says the LORD the God of Israel: The jar of meal will not be emptied and the jug of oil will not fail until the day that the LORD sends rain on the earth." [15]She went and did as Elijah said, so that she as well as he and her household ate for many days. [16]The jar of meal was not emptied, neither did the jug of oil fail, according to the word of the LORD that he spoke to Elijah.

In 1 Kings 17:8–16, we find the story of Elijah and the widow. It occurs in the midst of a three-year drought. God had sent Elijah into the wilderness where he was fed by the ravens and could drink water from the stream at the bottom of a ravine until the water dried up. God then sent Elijah to Zarephath, in the heart of Baal country on the Phoenician coast. God said Elijah would be fed and cared for by a widow in Zarephath.

Elijah entered into "enemy territory" where he became dependent on the hospitality not only of a stranger but of a foreigner and a person of different cultural values. Asking for a scarce drink of water, the widow responded according to the hospitality code of the desert and went to bring it to him. When Elijah called out asking for bread also, she told him she had only enough flour and oil to make one last meal for her son and herself. Her situation was desperate.

Elijah promised her, by "the LORD the God of Israel," that the flour and oil would last until the drought had ended. The widow, trusting Elijah's word and the word of the God of Israel, made him bread. Her supplies did last, enough for the widow's whole household.

The remarkable thing about this particular account of the widow and Elijah is that the hospitality required in the Law is not fulfilled by one of the people of the covenant, but instead by an outsider, a person of a rejected religion and culture. She demonstrated faithfulness to God's way yet was not one of the chosen people.

Her trust in the promise of Elijah and his God is striking. There was no reason why she should be open to his promise... this prophet came preaching against her religion and people. Yet she provided sustenance and shelter to Elijah...by this action, her own family and household were sustained.[38]

From Elijah and the widow we learn that an ever-widening circle of those who care and provide for one another is affirmed. Even the "enemy" or one who worships in different ways is part of the community of neighbors called on to offer care. With Elijah and the widow there was no insistence on conversion or rejection of her past. There was simply a bond in the affirmation of life and the community they had created, in their mutual need of each other, and in the presence of God in their midst.

Reflection

- In what ways has God used what little you had to bless someone in need?
- In what ways have you been blessed by someone who was very different from you?
- If we limit our hospitality, do we risk turning away someone sent by God?
- If we say yes to everyone, how will we keep what we offer from becoming diluted, more and more inadequate, and impersonal?

Sharing Our Story
Pamela Cress—Gulfport, Mississippi

Early on a Sunday morning in November, the phone rang in the home office of the pastor in Gulfport, Mississippi. Since the phone was double listed in the phone book for both the pastor's business and for the church, calls were not unusual at this time. The caller was a man who spoke in heavily accented broken English. He explained that he and his two cousins were at the Salvation Army shelter in town and wanted a ride to church. Arrangements were made for a couple of church members who lived north of town to drive to the shelter and pick up the men on their way to church. Since they all arrived at church just as services were beginning, there was time only for hasty introductions. Following the worship, a group of the congregation invited the men to dinner at a restaurant. During table conversation the men told their story.

They were from a small village on the western coast of Mexico and worked most of the year doing construction work in the Miami, Florida, area. While they usually sent most of their paychecks home for the care of their families, it was their habit to travel back to Mexico over the coldest months when work was limited in Florida. This time, as they had been traveling through Mississippi, their car had stopped working on the interstate. With only one of the three men able to speak much English, it had been very difficult to communicate with the tow truck driver who came to remove the car. They spoke of their confusion and fear in unfamiliar surroundings. The car had been taken to an auto repair business and they had been dropped at the Salvation Army shelter all at the suggestion of the tow truck driver. After a terrifying night at the shelter, they had decided to call the church in hope of finding some kind of help in dealing with their situation because they felt as if they were easy prey for someone who might be dishonest.

While living in Miami, they had been visited by Spanish-speaking elders from the Church of Jesus Christ of Latter-day Saints and had developed a friendly relationship. It was this church that they had thought they were calling. Although they had discovered that they had actually called a different church with a similar name, they said that they had no particular desire to pursue their original plan. They stated that they felt welcome among us and simply wanted some help with their car problem.

The three had been told that it would probably cost about $900 to repair the car at the shop where it had been taken. They had a little more than that much money on them but were afraid that it would not leave enough for gasoline to complete the trip. Additionally, they were concerned that the price was inflated. They had been so terrified that the money they had would be stolen from them at the shelter that they had not slept.

While the men rested at the home of the pastor, the church members devised a plan to help. The pastor's husband took two days off work in order to help. The cousins spent the night in the pastor's home. This time there was so much trust as they slept that the wallet with all of their money was left overnight on an end table after they finished showing family photos. The next morning, the church members picked up the disabled car and towed it behind a truck to the barn/shop of another church family. Following that effort, a small group of men worked steadily all day and through most of the next night to repair the car. Others made sure that all were fed and had plenty to drink. The Hispanic men were encouraged to help as they could. When the car repair was finally finished, the men were sent off with prayer, some road provisions, and many hugs.

In the years since then, Christmas cards have been exchanged and even some phone calls in expression of the bond of connection that was established during the time together.

Addressing Fear

Although church members know that making others feel at home is important, it's often approached as a job. It's not because we don't want to welcome new people; rather it's because many of us are uncomfortable meeting strangers. We're not sure what to say. Sometimes too—in all honesty—visitors may be so different from us that we're a bit afraid of them. The sad fact is the longer a person is a Christian, the more afraid they often become of non-Christians. They often have trouble relating to the life experiences of others.

In many respects, fear and distrust seem to have spread widely in our land. Symbols of openness are disappearing as we barricade ourselves from strangers in an effort to protect ourselves and our possessions. Electric door locks on cars, double locks on house doors, security alarms, guard dogs, lobby guards, security officers (even in our schools), increased numbers of police, and the military are just a few signs of our deep-seated fear of the stranger. We hide our money, lock our doors, chain our bikes, and look over our shoulders. We teach our children about "stranger danger," instilling within them a real sense of fear of others. News reports of break-ins, breakouts, and blackouts feed our fears. We are warned in the evening news reports to "be vigilant" in our awareness lest some unseen terror befall us. Unlike our predecessors from ancient times, we have come to view strangers more as potential enemies than as potential friends.

All our social institutions have been affected by the growth of fear in our society. Churches, once known as havens of refuge and houses of prayer, now lock the doors to the people to whom they claim to minister. Often, hospitality to the stranger has turned into hostility. Henri Nouwen remarked, "Our society seems to be increasingly full of fearful, defensive, aggressive people anxiously clinging to their property and inclined to look at their surrounding world with suspicion, always expecting an enemy to suddenly appear, intrude, and do harm."[39] However, by failing to come to know the stranger, we too often make that person an enemy rather than a friend. And as long as we let our Christian walk be governed by the fears that grip the rest of society, we will find ourselves unsettled by strangers and unable to make friendship the normal expectation when we encounter new people.

> **How ironic—the hostility and ill intentions we believe every stranger to possess actually radiate out as our *own* behaviors and attitudes when we confront the stranger. Could it be that strangers act unfriendly to us because they so often meet hostility instead of hospitality when they encounter someone new? Do strangers act like enemies because we treat them like enemies?**[40]

While our culture teaches us to be wary of strangers, we know that our best friends were once strangers to us. And we also should recognize that we are strangers to others. How others receive us, matters—at least to us. We need to remember that fact as we encounter those who are strange to us. Life is transformed when we see the stranger as potential friend.

Being fearful of strangers and the risk we encounter when we open ourselves to them is a common and natural occurrence. Many of us long for what we assume were "the good old days." We may mistakenly imagine that those days past were free of fears and doubt. That certainly hasn't been the case. Each day and age is filled with its own sense of uncertainty.

> **Martin Luther was sure that the Old Testament patriarchs and their children had found it safer and easier to offer hospitality to strangers than was the case for the Christians of the sixteenth century, for "there was not such a large number of vagabonds and scoundrels in the world as there is today." He warned households to be cautious "lest through lack of discretion they invite dangers for themselves." While patriarchs could receive "strangers as reverently as if God Himself were coming," "in our age, in these dregs of the world, there is such**

great wickedness, and there are such manifold instances of fraud and deceit that you do not know what to do for anyone."[41]

Hospitality will never be free from difficulty, but to sustain the practice, it is crucial to consider the well-being of hosts and guests. It is here that we quickly encounter struggles with limits and boundaries because physical and emotional strength, space, food, and other resources do not exist in endless supply. While God often supplies these resources miraculously, hosts still must make hard choices about how to distribute resources, expend energy, and focus ministry.[42]

Hospitality often involves risk—risk to one's health, one's property, even one's social standing. It involves great risk for the recipients also. Hospitality requires both host and guest to open doors to the unknown, to the unexpected. For hosts, it can mean opening one's doors to those who cannot always reciprocate, at least not in ways one can easily understand. For the guest, it requires putting one's life in another's hands without assurance that the host will either help or not harm. Hospitality, for both host and guest, involves loss, giving away one's life and security.[43]

In previous centuries, welcoming households were often quite large and active with many tasks to be completed. In truth, hospitality may have been easier for Abraham and our great-grandparents, not because people were less sinful in those days, but because the practice had a stronger moral claim and because households were larger. Never have households been so small, so frequently empty, and so separated from a larger community as they are today. The very private character of the contemporary home makes hospitality more difficult and more risky. Both hosts and guests are more afraid of being victimized when hospitality is completely hidden from the view of others.

One of the ways to reduce risk is to make hospitality more public—to share the task with others. This is not to suggest making hospitality less personal, but rather that welcome be initiated in a more public setting and sustained in less private places. This is both practical and wise. Personal hospitality cannot respond to every need. However, it can meet some needs; it can be a living demonstration of what is possible when people care. And like other shared tasks, when we work together, we can accomplish greater things.

Boundary Issues

The practice of hospitality as a spiritual discipline fosters a spirit of mutual dignity and sense of worth, generosity and compassion, love and respect, grace and mercy. It does not come, however, without its challenges and difficulties for individuals, families, and congregations. A lifestyle of hospitality requires difficult choices about how to distribute limited resources, expend energy and time, and focus ministry. Hosts will experience guests whose sole purpose is to take advantage of the open heart and open home. Others will frustrate those who would help because their great need cannot be met by the host.

These are real concerns, and it is important that we not become victims of those who seek to use us and our resources in ways that are not life-enhancing or spirit-building. Without periods of rest and renewal, host families, individuals, and congregations can become weary, relationships can become strained, as limits are stretched and family cohesiveness is taxed. Guidelines, rules, and policies are important in setting boundaries that preserve the dignity of all, foster mutual respect, and give space for privacy, renewal, and rest. Having the maturity to learn how to love unconditionally within healthy social, psychological, and spiritual limitations and boundaries is the heart of the gospel.[44]

It is never easy to find the balance between rest, relaxation, and nourishment on one hand, and generosity and availability on the other. Only the Holy Spirit can teach us to love ourselves sufficiently to be able to give our lives as totally and completely as possible. If we are not well, in good shape, joyful, and nourished, we will not give life to others; instead, we will communicate sadness and emptiness.[45]

While we are instructed to open our hearts to God's people, we know too often that the people who become known for their generous response to strangers often find increasing numbers of strangers at their door—whether it is the door to a home, church, or community business. Sometimes, the numbers or the frequency of guests increases so quickly that hosts find themselves burdened, overwhelmed, and stretched to their limits. We may find our energy, resources, space, identity, generosity, and sense of cohesion strained. Faced with such pressures, hosts and host communities either work out guidelines or give up hospitality.

Establishing boundaries is an essential component of successful, sustained hospitality. We should not be afraid to think through these issues and decide before a guest arrives just what our limits will be. Addressing issues about how space and other resources of time, food, and money will be used is vital for hosts. We may understand that boundaries are troublesome in the context of hospitality for a number of reasons. By definition, hospitality is gracious and generous. Limiting hospitality seems to undermine what is fundamental to the practice. However, by thinking through our actions and our limits, we are more likely to be able to extend our acts of welcoming beyond just meeting an immediate need. In fact, setting boundaries helps define what individuals, a household, family, church, or community hold precious.

Opening our hearts and our doors to let others in requires a measure of courage, faith, and discipline. Learning to release or limit the fear we carry regarding encounters with strangers is an important step for disciples. Yet we must also be tuned in to that inner voice or gut feeling or instinct that warns us when danger is near—danger that appears not only in physical threats but also in emotional or spiritual jeopardy. To ignore this inner warning, often spells harm. However, learning when to relax a set of fears to trust in the welcoming of a guest can open wide our experience with that person in a way that God blesses. To be a hostage to the fear keeps us from the potential blessing.

Welcome is one of the signs that a community is alive. To invite others, whether strangers or visitors, to live with us is a sign that we aren't afraid, that we have a treasure of truth and of peace to share. However, a community that refuses to welcome—whether through fear, weariness, insecurity, a desire to cling to comfort, or just because it is fed up with visitors—is dying spiritually.[46]

Balancing Our Values and the Needs of Our Guests

Receptivity is only one side of hospitality. The other side is confrontation. Being receptive doesn't mean that we become doormats, allowing guests to do anything they want to our homes or to us. True welcoming space has to have boundaries, for everyone's sake. Welcoming our guests while hiding who we really are and what our values are is like welcoming our guests to an empty house. Guests may get to do anything they want, but it can be lonely. There's no point of reference, no one to talk to, no one to bounce ideas off, and no point of orientation. It may begin to feel like a ghost house.

When we want to be really hospitable we not only have to receive strangers but also to confront them by an unambiguous

> **presence, not hiding ourselves behind neutrality but showing our ideas, opinions and life style clearly and distinctly. No real dialogue is possible between somebody and a nobody. We can enter into communication with the other only when our life choices, attitudes and viewpoints offer the boundaries that challenge strangers to become aware of their own position and to explore it critically.**[47]

It is important that when entertaining nonbelieving guests, we don't forego our normal religious observances. For example, if our custom is to pray at meal times, saying grace over a meal when nonbelievers are present shows our guests what's important to us and what our beliefs are. Also, standards we have for our homes and the church should be relaxed within limits that are not harmful to our integrity or to others. We can't assume that strangers know our customs, but we can sometimes go too far in our accommodation of strangers and guests. For instance, if we do not smoke in our home or in our church, we should expect guests to honor that boundary as well.

Offering hospitality requires that we allow a place for uncertainty, contingency, human tragedy, and unexpected surprises. If we expect it to be easy to welcome strangers—that it will always involve competent hosts and grateful guests—we will be disappointed and will grow discouraged very quickly.

Hospitality is hard work. One real danger is underestimating what it may cost us in time, resources, effort, and satisfaction. However, if we are genuinely concerned about the needs of strangers, offering hospitality requires courage. It involves not only a willingness to take some risks in welcoming others, but it requires the kind of courage that lives close to our limits, continually presses against the possible, and yet is always aware of the incompleteness and the inadequacy of our responses.

If we do decide to extend the hand of hospitality to strangers and friends, we should know that we will not remain unchanged. By welcoming strangers, the community's identity is always being challenged and revised, if only slightly. New faces in our lives and churches bring new energy, gifts, skills, and needs. Our ministry will change because of these new aspects of our growing family. That is exactly what should happen. When strangers are welcomed in, especially if they come in significant numbers or if they are quite different from the welcoming community, there will be some strains on identity. But we know that the community will be transformed by the people it welcomes. Those communities that welcomed us (our families, schools, jobs, clubs, churches, small groups, sports teams, and so on) have all changed because of our inclusion. The same will be true when we welcome and include others.

Sharing ourselves with others is a precious gift and a special opportunity to share Christ with others. Families and congregations who are shaped by deep Christian faith and strong love for one another can offer an extraordinary gift in welcoming others into their homes and churches. By living our lives in front of our guests, we provide a model of a healthy family and community, warts and all. This is authentic sharing.

Surviving Wear and Tear and Fatigue

Engaging in hospitality changes everyone who is involved in the act—the givers, receivers, and observers. This involvement can also change physical things. While the basic principles of stewardship encourage us to care for and maintain our gifts and resources, continual efforts to protect and preserve these possessions can have a stifling effect on hospitality. We must acknowledge that some things will be broken and other things will disappear or wear out when we open our lives to others.

Sharing Our Story
Paul Snethen—Des Moines, Iowa

Our latest guest provides an interesting story. Deb was beginning a new job and needed a place to stay for a few weeks as she went through job training. Deb only stayed a week because she was more homesick than she thought, and the 150-mile round trip seemed to be a better option. We enjoyed Deb's company the few days she stayed with us.

We are blessed with a garage that is capable of housing four cars if tucked in carefully. Parking three cars inside is easy. However, on the last day, Deb was so excited to leave she turned too soon and damaged her pickup and the garage door track and jamb. I felt bad for her knowing she would feel so bad for the damage to our garage, which I repaired in about twenty minutes. The repairs to her truck would not be so simple. We received a thank-you note and an additional apology a few days later.

We had another friend call as he was passing through and he had the same problem the next morning as he left, catching his mirror on the jamb and scratching a line in the paint from the door jamb just above where Deb had removed a piece of the jamb seal.

I see these "injuries" each day as I go in and out of the garage and I remember both visits. Although the jamb is damaged, it is more like a signature and a reminder of good company, good conversations, and pleasant associations. I thank Deb and Ed for leaving their marks to enable me to remember their coming, staying, and going; especially the coming and staying, if only for a short time. They are both welcome back. For I have learned that strangers only stay strangers until you get acquainted.

Many people who practice the kind of hospitality proclaimed in the gospel describe it as both the best and the hardest thing they have ever done. In their experience, its difficulty and its joys lie close together. They find it to be the "best thing" because they sense God's presence so frequently in the practice. In essence, they witness small miracles and discover how scripture and prayer come alive. Hospitality is wonderful because it is filled with unexpected blessings, because it is fun, and because of the opportunities it provides to become friends with so many kinds of people.

Hospitality is difficult because it involves hard work and causes us to risk. People wear out and struggle with limits. Many of us place a high value on control, planning, and efficiency. But hospitality is unpredictable and often inefficient. We may desire measurable results and completed tasks but the "results" of hospitality are impossible to quantify and the work is rarely finished. It is here that we must learn to let go of our "business as usual" approach of understanding the results of our hospitality. We must offer our gifts and then get out of the way of the results.

The act of release or sending forth includes letting go of the outcome of the practices of hospitality. The practices of hospitality are independent of their outcomes. "One lives hospitably without any guarantee of a payoff. The sick person may die, the stranger may misuse the resources shared, or the hospitality offered may not be honored. Desire for a particular consequence of hospitality must be released."[48]

Because hospitality can be so demanding, we need to find a renewing rhythm of work, rest, and worship. Without periods of rest and solitude, and without access to spiritual nourishment, we wear out quickly. It is part of the balance of the giving and receiving, the doing and being. It is impossible to sustain hospitality without attention to both spiritual and physical needs. As with any discipline, it, too, requires purposeful attention and effort to sustain. Those who offer hospitality find that the practice itself is nourishing. We discover that a life of hospitality brings us life. Fed by the practice through the guests who come and through the gifts they bring, in a mysterious way we are also nourished by God's grace and love, which infuse hospitality.

Practical Helps for Congregations

Consider the following suggestions. Make note of one or two that your congregation can work to implement in the coming weeks.

General Suggestions

- Have greeting time early in the service.
- Provide pictures of people in various locations around the facility. People love to see themselves and people they know in photographs.
- Identify special parking for expectant mothers, parents with small children, guests/members with special needs.
- Ensure restrooms and nursery facilities are in good condition before guests' arrival.
- Phone the first-time guest by Tuesday following the Sunday visit.
- Send a personal, handwritten letter from the pastor to the first-time guest.
- Provide something delivered to the doorstep of the first-time guest, if possible within twenty-four hours following first visit.
- Ensure that all written announcements and publications are complete and written with guests in mind. Provide all the pertinent details: who, what, when, where, how, how much/often.
- Have a visible information center for guests to connect with. Staff this center each Sunday and keep it stocked and orderly.

- Start new ministry teams or groups often. Despite their best intentions, ongoing groups have a tendency to become cliquish. Newcomers are far more likely to feel comfortable joining something new.
- Avoid pet projects that only involve a few people.
- Be mindful of ministries that no longer serve their purpose. Don't continue to invest energy in trying to keep a dying program alive.

Equip and Affirm

- Intentionally include newcomers in leadership.
- Reinforce the need for openness in leadership roles with a rotation system.
- Experienced leaders should be encouraged to recruit a co-leader and mentor that person.
- Encourage members to think of their involvements in the context of their personal spiritual growth. Help them chart a deliberate plan for spiritual growth.
- Move away from the "committee" mindset, to the more collaborative and interactive "ministry team" mindset.
- Make time for affirmation and appreciation. Develop a systematic plan to publicly recognize all groups and ministries teams over the course of the year.
- Say "Thank you!" often.

Caring for Children and Youth

- See children and youth as participants in ministry, not merely objects of ministry.
- Teach children to pray. Encourage them to share joys and concerns and to participate in prayer.
- Don't guess at the needs of children and youth. Listen to children. Solicit input and feedback from children and youth themselves, not just from parents and adult leaders.
- Give children and youth real responsibilities.

- Use children in worship and worship planning.
- Give children and youth meaningful and visible roles as worship participants.
- Showcase the work/artwork of children and youth.
- Celebrate the arrival of new babies.
- Include at least one hymn every Sunday that children love and can sing with the congregation.
- Have children serve alongside other greeters and ushers.
- Provide small children entering worship a small activity packet with soft, clean, quiet activities.
- Make special times for children and their families to visit the sanctuary, to ask questions, and to learn the stories behind symbols.
- Make your space child-friendly. Nursery and classrooms should be clean, safe, sanitary, and visually appealing to children and their parents.
- When planning for children and youth ministry, remember that relationships are more important than programs. Create ways for each person to experience a sense of belonging.
- Include children and youth in an active role in the leadership and decision making of the church.
- Host seminars on parenting.
- Integrate "service learning" into Christian education to teach discipleship.
- Have a Sunday morning class focused on family concerns.
- Offer a support group for new parents.
- Have an annual family retreat.
- Pair an adult class or group with each children's class to forge intergenerational bonds. The adults can provide support and encouragement and help with special activities.
- Give nicely printed invitations to the baptismal family so they can invite their friends to attend.
- Follow up after vacation church school programs or other

events. Be purposeful in getting contact information for follow-up invitations.

- Adopt a local school. Be available to provide support to students, staff, and parents.
- Develop a tutoring or mentoring ministry.

Chapter 6

Given to Hospitality: Beyond Soup and Bread, Blanket and Bed

> **Each disciple needs a spiritual home. You are called to build that home and care for it, but also to share equally in the outreaching ministries of the church. In that way the gospel may be sent to other souls also yearning for a spiritual resting place.**
>
> **—Doctrine and Covenants 162:7d**

Scripture Focus—Paul's Letter to Philemon —Verses 1–25

[1]Paul, a prisoner of Christ Jesus, and Timothy our brother,
To Philemon our dear friend and coworker, [2]to Apphia our sis-
ter, to Archippus our fellow soldier, and to the church in your
house: [3]Grace to you and peace from God our Father and the
Lord Jesus Christ.

[4]When I remember you in my prayers, I always thank my
God [5]because I hear of your love for all the saints and your
faith toward the Lord Jesus. [6]I pray that the sharing of your
faith may become effective when you perceive all the good

that we may do for Christ. [7]I have indeed received much joy
and encouragement from your love, because the hearts of the
saints have been refreshed through you, my brother.

[8]For this reason, though I am bold enough in Christ to
command you to do your duty, [9]yet I would rather appeal
to you on the basis of love—and I, Paul, do this as an old
man, and now also as a prisoner of Christ Jesus. [10]I am ap-
pealing to you for my child, Onesimus, whose father I have
become during my imprisonment. [11]Formerly he was use-
less to you, but now he is indeed useful both to you and
to me. [12]I am sending him, that is, my own heart, back to
you. [13]I wanted to keep him with me, so that he might be
of service to me in your place during my imprisonment for
the gospel; [14]but I preferred to do nothing without your con-
sent, in order that your good deed might be voluntary and
not something forced. [15]Perhaps this is the reason he was
separated from you for a while, so that you might have him
back forever, [16]no longer as a slave but more than a slave,
a beloved brother—especially to me but how much more to
you, both in the flesh and in the Lord.

[17]So if you consider me your partner, welcome him as you
would welcome me. [18]If he has wronged you in any way, or
owes you anything, charge that to my account. [19]I, Paul, am
writing this with my own hand: I will repay it. I say nothing
about your owing me even your own self. [20]Yes, brother, let
me have this benefit from you in the Lord! Refresh my heart
in Christ. [21]Confident of your obedience, I am writing to you,
knowing that you will do even more than I say.

[22]One thing more—prepare a guest room for me, I am hop-
ing through your prayers to be restored to you.

[23]Epaphras, my fellow prisoner in Christ Jesus, sends greet-
ings to you, [24]and so do Mark, Aristarchus, Demas, and Luke,
my fellow workers.

25 The grace of the Lord Jesus Christ be with your spirit.

In order to interpret the intent of Paul's letter to Philemon, the reader is required to reconstruct the situation this letter presupposes; but to do that, we must depend on the letter itself. Paul is writing this letter from prison. He has been joined by Onesimus, who is the slave of Philemon. It seems that Onesimus has converted to the gospel while he was with Paul. How Onesimus encountered Paul is unclear. Perhaps he ran away from his master, or he may have been sent by Philemon to serve Paul in prison. What matters is that the encounter has changed both Paul and Onesimus.

Paul's letter is intended to be presented by Onesimus upon his return to Philemon and to register a plea on Onesimus's behalf. It is not completely clear what Paul is asking in this letter. Perhaps he is asking Philemon to receive Onesimus back as a servant and forgive his transgressions. Perhaps he is asking Philemon to send Onesimus back to him in prison. But it may be that he is encouraging Philemon to not only receive Onesimus back but to also free him as he is now a brother in Christ as are Paul and the others mentioned in the letter. While Paul's encouragement is strongly rendered, the decision is left to Philemon himself.

This letter has played a leading role in the history of Christian social ethics. It speaks to more than the attitude toward the institution of slavery. It speaks about taking risks to do what is right even when we are wronged. What should Philemon do? Can he welcome Onesimus home as a brother in Christ? What might this do to other slaves or servants who may take advantage of this and fake a conversion in order to be freed, too? How will this affect the relationship between each of them?

If we take this as an example for today, we must consider the effect of welcoming people into our communities after they have had a change of heart. What if that person has hurt or caused us grief in the past? We may want to respond initially with actions that are not becoming of our calling as disciples. We may encounter difficulties separating our former struggles with the transformed person now before us. It places a challenging obstacle in our paths—one that calls for courage and trust to choose a path that may be against our immediate human nature.

Paul's approach seems to be to regard other Christians as family members, calling them brother and sister. Because Onesimus is now a Christian, Paul calls him brother as well. This letter encourages Philemon to do the difficult thing. To Paul it is the right thing.

Reflection

- When have you been called on to do something difficult for the right reason?
- When was a time you had difficulty embracing another as a sister or brother in Christ because of a painful infraction?
- What implications for the practice of hospitality does Paul's letter to Philemon have for us today?
- What implications does this letter have to how Christians receive and minister to those who have been in prison? Or to those who have converted from past corrupt or criminal behaviors?

The Power to Respond

Modern households usually include two small instruments that resemble one another in appearance. They are actually very different in their functions. One is a thermometer, the other a thermostat. The thermometer simply displays the temperature it measures. The thermostat also measures and displays a temperature reading; however, it also has the capacity to make a difference by responding to a need. It slowly and steadily changes the climate by turning on the furnace or the air conditioner, depending on which is needed. In the life of local congregations, hospitality ministries resemble the thermostat. No other program emphasis has as much potential for making a difference as hospitality.

There is power in being able to offer a response to a need. In fact, responding to needs by offering a portion of God's love to someone else is the power of ministry. It's more than just saying the words or believing the words are true. It is in the action, the doing, the responding that love is shared and lives are changed. After studying a French Protestant community that offered hospitality to thousands of Jewish refugees during World War II, author Philip Hallie concluded, "Deeds speak the language of the great virtues far better than words do.... Words limp outside the gates of the mystery of compassion for strangers."[49]

Hospitality is not merely a subheading under ministry. Hospitality is a climate of inclusiveness. It is people-centered, not program-centered. It is a way of being the church. It is the church practicing what it preaches. It is how congregations share their faith in God's great generosity revealed in Jesus.[50]

Acts of hospitality are dynamic. They occur in a variety of settings and they have hidden strength and power within them. We would be wrong to assume that gifts of hospitality flow in one direction only. Hospitality is a two-way street. Those who give often receive far more in return. Those who receive at times are offered a chance to share in their own special ways. Sometimes those standing outside and observing the events of hospitality are blessed and inspired to give as well. In the giving and receiving, all are blessed. A small example is found in the following story.

Dia and John are young adults in Jonesboro, Arkansas. They have four young children including one set of twins. One child had been inviting a friend to church. Then, the friend's whole family came to church.

John and Dia often go out to lunch after church, so they took the friend's whole family out to lunch as well.

Wayne, a man who loves to cook, noticed this and was concerned that it must cost a great deal for John and Dia to take everyone out to eat. The next Sunday, he came to church with a big pot of food all prepared to give to John and Dia so they could take their kids, the friend, and the friend's family all home to supper.

It is important for us as disciples to be aware of the environments and surroundings in which we find ourselves. Some have discovered that not only are unknown needs present around them, but also that hidden skills and abilities are uncovered when a response is offered to a friend or stranger in need. If we find ourselves unaware of people in need, perhaps we need to open our eyes and ears to those around us in more intentional ways. We also need to be purposeful about praying for opportunities to offer acts of welcome and caring to neighbors, friends, or a stranger in need. Following is a list of suggestions for how to start:

- Be intentional now and then about including a few extra people at meal times. Invite a lonely neighbor to share a meal.
- Invite additional people to participate in family holiday celebrations and special events.
- If you are single, join with another person or with larger families to share in the work of preparing meals and making a place for hospitality.
- Assist someone recovering from surgery.
- Provide transportation to someone who doesn't drive.

- Host a small-group meeting for Bible study or support.
- Befriend someone new to town, perhaps an immigrant.
- Establish a coffee house in your congregation or a renewal center that creates a comfortable environment for conversation and refreshment.
- If you teach English as a Second Language (ESL) courses, make your classes havens of hospitality.
- View telephone calls as a place for hospitality. Phone calls often sustain crucial human relationships and can be an important way to care for one another.

Seeing Jesus at Work

Our contemporary situation is similar in some regard to the early Christian context in which the normative understandings and practices of hospitality were developed. Like the early church, we find ourselves in a fragmented and multicultural society that yearns for connection, belonging, identity, and meaning. In our mobile, self-oriented society, we encounter disturbing levels of mistrust, loneliness, alienation, and estrangement. In a culture that appears at times to be hostile to life itself, those who reject violence and embrace life have the opportunity to bear powerful witness.

At a basic level we understand that God is at work in the world. We need to truly believe that. We also need to trust that our sometimes small but significant moves participate in that work. When we welcome another person, we welcome Christ. When we share with a stranger, we share with Christ. Likewise, when we neglect or reject another, in effect we are neglecting and rejecting Christ. We need to learn to see Jesus in those we serve, and pray that those we serve are able to see Jesus in us and through our actions.

Our actions and involvement are critical elements of Christian discipleship. That is partly why the church is often referred to as the body of Christ in the world. It is through us that the work is done and the world is changed. What we do matters—to the world and to God. What we give makes a difference.

Henri Nouwen noted that "we will never believe that we have anything to give unless there is someone who is able to receive. Indeed, we discover our gifts in the eyes of the receiver."[51] It is true, we may understand the concept of hospitality at a certain safe and sterile level, but we make a habit of hospitality when we remember how much Jesus is present in the practice. To review his life and teachings in scripture is the best place to remember.

Jesus and the stranger stand outside, asking individuals and communities to enlarge our borders and to share our resources. We eagerly and easily share with friends; those we know, trust, and acknowledge; those with similar interests, abilities, and resources. However, when we welcome the stranger, the unknown, the marginal person, or the person who has wronged us, they help us to remember that each of us is also an alien and a stranger, welcomed initially by God's generous invitation and dependent on others, too.

Hospitality practiced in the homes of Christian people is a key foundation for hospitality in the church. In effect, the front door of the home can be the side door of the church. Today it is crucial for us to recover both household and church as key settings for hospitality. We know that a welcoming place is rich with stories, rituals, and a history. Homes and congregations are or can be such places. In them, people are valued and lives are nurtured. These are never simply physical spaces, but they are places alive with commitments and relationships. In these places, lives are developed and changed. In these places, great power and responsibility exist to shape lives. However, we recognize that some hospitality concerns cannot be handled adequately by home or church, and we must also recognize the important role government and large institutions now play in provision and protection. We should take care not to minimize the necessity of some structural supports for the poor and refugees. But personal hospitality has an important place in contemporary life, and the central tenets of Christian hospitality still challenge contemporary institutions to make their practices more humane and person-oriented.[52]

Acts of hospitality—large and small—can produce dramatic results. Sometimes these results go unknown or unnoticed. And because some effects are only noticed over time, we must wait for the events to unfold and for the impact of those events to be felt and shared. Sometimes we find that acts of hospitality shape more than just the direct recipients of the gift. Sometimes the gift that is shared today can shape countless generations to come. We can experience such change because God's people dared to share.

Sharing Our Story—Saved by the Grace of God

One July afternoon in 1932, three children—two girls and their younger brother—sat on the top step of their front porch in Independence, Missouri, wondering what to do next. The front door opened, and out came their father. He walked past them, out to the sidewalk in front of the house. "Hey, Daddy," shouted five-year-old Dorothy, "Where you goin'?" Their father looked back, smiled, and said, "To get you kids some ice cream. I'll be back soon!"

Frankie, the younger sister, age three, squealed with delight at the prospect of ice cream on such a hot day. Their little brother, Dickie, was only two, but ice cream was already his favorite food.

If those children had sat there waiting for their ice cream a whole day, or a week, they would never have tasted it. Their daddy was gone, forever.

Their mother, Audrey, joined them on the porch. Together they wondered what had happened to their "man of the house." After Audrey had put her children to bed for the night, her neighbors, Margie and May, came to inquire about her and the children. These neighbors had helped Audrey and her family before during difficult times. They had also shared many good times together, but expected that trouble might be brewing for the young family.

The father, Frank, was unstable, often gone from home for days without explanation. He'd get his weekly pay on Friday afternoons, but often did not come home until Sunday evenings, usually without any money and not able to tell why. But on that hot July day, he just vanished. Margie and May were very worried about the situation. They cared for the children as much as they could, and counseled with Audrey about what to do.

Audrey traveled to Kansas City to inquire about Frank at the company where he worked. No one seemed to know where Frank had gone. She returned home with a heavy heart. She and her husband owed the neighborhood grocer more than $500 for food, long ago bought and eaten. Audrey had no employment and no prospects for finding work. Even if she were to find work, who would care for her children? How could she ever pay the debt to the grocer?

She phoned her father, Henry, in Chicago. He arrived by train a few weeks later, and began to help his daughter plan what to do. A tip from Frank's sister led them to California. Henry, his daughter, and her three children boarded a train for the West. They'd learned that Frank was working in San Francisco.

They arrived in San Francisco and rented two small rooms in a dreary tenement near the waterfront. While Henry cared for his grandchildren, Audrey found the office building where Frank was supposed to be and went to ask about her husband. The receptionist exclaimed, "We'd like to know where he's gone, too. Frank is our mystery man. We hope he comes back soon. He's got some of our equipment to sell, and we want *it* back, but not *him*!"

Anxious and perplexed, Audrey left the office. With tears in her eyes, she walked slowly toward Golden Gate Park, and as luck would have it, she saw Frank near the park's entrance. He was shabbily dressed, unshaven, and red-eyed. She smelled liquor on his breath. She spoke briefly with him, and he promised to return to her and the children. They made plans for the next day. She went to meet him, but he failed to show up. She never saw or heard from him again.

Meanwhile, all three of her children had contracted measles. Audrey and her father arranged for money for food with a local relief agency for a few days, until the children were well enough to travel back home. One evening, just after sunset, Audrey stood on the shore of the Pacific Ocean. The huge waves crashed over the rocks nearby. She was at the lowest point of despair she'd ever known. She asked herself, "Why not walk out into that pounding surf until my hat just floats away?" In the next breath, she told herself, "Time to go see about the kids."

That momentous decision changed everything for her and for them. Audrey, her father, and her three children boarded the bus for home. Along the way, she made contact with friends in Salt Lake City, who offered to parent the two girls for as long as it might take Audrey to find a job and get proper housing for her family. So Henry, Audrey, and Dickie continued the bus trip to Missouri. Henry arranged to take his grandson to Chicago to live with his uncle Emerson and aunt Nellie and their two children. Their plan was for Audrey to find work and stabilize her household so she could bring all her children back home permanently.

During the following year, Audrey struggled to find employment, only occasionally working temporary jobs in restaurants as a waitress. She was making no real progress toward reuniting with her children. Her education and vocational skills were limited. She concluded that the only way her children could ever have a home would be for her to adopt them out through the civil court system. She spoke with her friends Margie and May of her final plan. These two courageous women intervened immediately. Their proposal: "Audrey, bring your children back here, and move in and live with us until you can make a home for them. We cannot bear to see you lose your family like this."

During the summer of 1933, Dorothy and Frankie arrived from Salt Lake City, and Dickie, accompanied by his uncle Emerson, arrived several weeks later. He has always remembered that magic moment of being welcomed and embraced by his two sisters, his mother, and his two "new mothers," Margie and May. That crowded apartment was meant to be his temporary home. As the weeks and months and years rolled on, however, he came to know their home as his own. His mother finally found a steady job, but beyond that she found two trusted friends, who in turn came to love the three children as family. They all moved from the apartment to a house, and then to a larger house, as the children grew to adulthood.

Margie was a member of the RLDS Stone Church congregation. May belonged to First Christian Church. Audrey and her three children attended First Presbyterian Church for several years. Margie, who owned a car, took everyone to their respective churches on Sundays and went on alone to Stone Church. There she prayed that Audrey and her children one day might become part of the Stone Church congregation. And over the next six to seven years, it happened. In June 1941, all five of them were baptized in the Stone Church font. The children became active in choirs, youth groups, and Sunday school. They found "friends for a lifetime." Most important, they grew up together in the same family. Life was not always peaceful and serene, but they knew the blessings of being welcomed and valued in a place that soon became their spiritual home.

Long after those three children grew up to establish their own vocations and families, the three "mothers" continued to maintain their own household, and with that, their lifelong loyalties to one another, to the children, and to the grandchildren who came along to bless their lives with joys and surprises.

The three mothers and two sisters attended Dick's graduation from Graceland College in 1952, giving him a highly valued gift: the three scriptural books of the church, bound in rich leather, with his name printed in gold on each of the front covers. To this day, Richard Howard, former church historian, still wonders at the long-term effects of the welcoming spirit in church and family, and in the church-as-family.

A stone dropped in a pond sends ripples out to the edges. Margie's and May's blessed act of welcome and hospitality in 1933—repeated and extended over many years—continues to ripple God's grace and compassion into every corner of the life of this boy-become-man, to this very day!

—Richard P. Howard

Basic Equipment

Hospitality should be offered for its own sake because that is what God expects of disciples. Yet if we're honest, we know that through such acts of caring and sharing, our lives are opened to someone else. We often share ourselves in ways that display who and what we care about. Our practices, opinions, beliefs, behaviors, hopes, and dreams are revealed through such activities. So we know that engaging in the act of welcoming guests holds potential opportunities for witnessing of Christ's love for the world.

Recognizing the importance of welcoming guests, the Community of Christ has developed a series of resources that focus on the various aspects of welcoming and witnessing. The Witnessing Disciple Series is a collection of resources designed to assist, equip, and encourage members and congregations in accomplishing the tasks and primary calling associated with sharing Jesus Christ with others. These resources are designed for congregations, members, and those who are seeking a relationship with God and the church.

The resource *A Witnessing Community: A Basic Guide to Congregational Ministry* has been acknowledged as the foundational guide for assisting congregations in the Community of Christ in preparing facilities, budgets, and members to receive and welcome guests. This resource, along with others found in the Missionary Tool Kit, provides assistance to congregational members and seekers in understanding the nature and work of the church through witnessing ministries.

The Witnessing Disciple Series continues to expand its focus by providing resources that assist with developing and sharing a personal testimony, identifying neighbors and friends with whom to share in home missionary meetings, providing group support for witnessing efforts, supplying helpful materials to give to friends about the Community of Christ and what it means to be a disciple, and encouraging the reluctant disciple to overcome fears about outreach as they open themselves to friends, neighbors, and to God's guiding Spirit.

It is important for disciples to connect with these tools and other good ideas that will enhance welcoming and witnessing encounters. Start with understanding what a stranger, guest, friend, or seeker may be experiencing when they are in an unfamiliar situation. One way to do this is to reflect on your experiences as a guest or stranger: What made you feel comfortable, valued, safe? What communicated to you that you were inconvenient or in the way? What is it about certain people and places that make you feel renewed and nourished?

When someone enters a new space, three questions surface and are processed very quickly. If people cannot answer these three questions easily and effortlessly, they may choose to leave. The questions are:

- Do I feel safe?—Safety may include physical and/or emotional considerations.
- Do I feel welcome?—Welcoming includes allowing the guest to enter and engage as they are ready.
- What is expected of me?—Guests wonder if they can help themselves or if they need help or permission from someone already connected.[53]

Understanding these questions is important for church members and leaders. Working to provide positive answers to these questions in our congregational settings will better enable our worship and fellowship spaces to be welcoming, witnessing places. Take some time to reflect on the following questions. It may be most helpful to record answers to these questions and share them with someone else.

- Is your church hard to find? Does a new person need directions or an ad in a paper or phone book to know about you?
- What might people driving by your church building know about what goes on there?
- Is it easy to know where to park and go in?
- Is the way to enter your church obvious? Is your primary entrance easily identified?
- Are all the entrance doors to the building unlocked?
- Are members available in the parking lot and at the doors to help with umbrellas, kids, and elderly guests?

- When do worship services or other activities begin? Is that information posted and accessible?
- Where does the worship take place? Is that information posted and accessible?
- Do you advertise in the local paper or phone book or on a Web site? Is it updated regularly?
- Is there an answering machine with times, directions, contact information? Is it monitored regularly?
- Once you're inside the building, are there appropriate signs to point the way so guests can locate the restrooms, nursery, classrooms, sanctuary, office, etc.?
- Is there someone to greet and welcome guests?
- What do you do as a congregation to make people feel welcome from the parking lot to the sanctuary? How can this be improved?
- What do you, as individuals, do to make people feel welcome from the parking lot to the sanctuary? What can you do to improve this welcome?
- What are the benefits of small groups in our church? How are these benefits shared or not shared with newcomers?
- Recall your first time in a new Bible study class, school, or new job. How did you feel? What helped you eventually feel at home?
- What do you do as a congregation to make people feel welcome in a small group? How can this be improved?
- What do you, as individuals, do to make people feel welcome in a small group? How can you help to improve this?
- How can you prepare your congregation to receive guests?

As with most things, the human touch or encounter cannot be replaced and should not be undervalued. In hospitality and witnessing, it is the human resource that is the critical element. Without this component—person to person—sharing Christ's message is not likely to occur. It falls to each of us as disciples to be the conduit for inviting, welcoming, witnessing, and discipling. Yet disciples can equip themselves with other tools to assist in the ministry. The Witnessing Disciple Series contains some of these tools. Other tools congregations may utilize include the creation of guest invitational and informational resources. These items may be Web sites, brochures, welcome cards, letters or postcards of invitation or of recognition, newsletters, bulletin inserts, door hangers, guest packets, tracts, information centers, surveys, stickers, bookmarks, magnets, mugs, pens, pencils, an inquirers' class, testimonies, prayer, and a nearly endless list of other ideas. Go to the Community of Christ Web site at *www.CofChrist.org/seventy/resources.asp* for helpful suggestions and adjustable templates.

Congregations are encouraged to be creative in what they design and offer to guests. A coordinated effort to create and distribute an elaborate guest packet should not take the place of equipping congregational members with an understanding of providing a hospitable welcome. Without the personal touch, all we may have is pretty paper with fancy wording. The tool may say the right thing, but it will lack the most important element—that personal connection.

Moving Forward

Many exciting ideas, concepts, insights, and challenges have been shared throughout this resource. We know by reflecting on the scriptural teachings presented here that the topic of offering hospitality and extending God's welcome to others was and continues to be a priority for God's people. Christian disciples are called to meet needs and to do unto others as if we were meeting Christ's needs and doing unto him. We are reminded to balance between "doing" and "being" activities. We are learning to recognize and remember the guest who is among us. We are challenged to act for right even when we have been wronged. We are learning also about the power to trust God for outcomes to the little we have to offer. And through the sharing of our stories these important concepts come into sharper focus. Through them we recall the blessings we have received through the love and nurture of others along the way.

All of this learning and remembering and trusting and sharing are vital to our individual and collective growth as Christian disciples. It is through actions and practice that disciples grow and develop. When we work and learn together, we are richly blessed. Hospitality often is accomplished in small steps by individuals, but it is to community that we have been called and to which we belong, and it is in community that the body of Christ, the church, functions at its best.

This resource is merely a tool to spark further practice, study, action, and growth. In it, a multitude of ideas and suggestions have been offered, some of which may require further study and reflection. It is hoped that you and the members of your community of Christ will focus together on a few and bravely take a step toward investing in the promises of hospitality.

Individually, as leaders, or as an entire congregational family, spend time with the *Discover and Share Your Gifts* inventory found at the end of this resource. Align the discovery of those gifts with congregational goals and mission. Consider a mentoring program for those with similar gifts and interests. Identify a couple of areas as a beginning focus. And remember to focus your prayer efforts on hospitality opportunities. These opportunities are present throughout our daily lives. We sometimes need to have prayerful focus to be reminded to look for and to see opportunities that are before us awaiting our response. This is Christ's call to us—to share his gospel and open our hearts to receive and share God's blessings with others. The Community of Christ is called to share—specifically, to share the peace of Jesus Christ with the world. Hospitality and welcoming ministries are important avenues to achieve this sharing. What you share today will become a multiplied blessing tomorrow.

Appendix

Discover and Share Your Gifts[54]

Gifts Discovery Questionnaire

Directions: Circle only one answer for each statement.

If the statement is mostly false, circle 1.
If the statement is somewhat true, circle 3.
If the statement is consistently true, circle 5.

1.	I know when and to whom to delegate important responsibility.	1	3	5
2.	There is positive response to my leadership in new congregations or ministries.	1	3	5
3.	I am strongly aware of the presence of the Spirit in my life.	1	3	5
4.	I believe that God is blessing me with a unique capability to work with my hands to create things of beauty and utility.	1	3	5
5.	I can usually recognize whether a teaching is of godly origin.	1	3	5
6.	I have dreams and/or visions that I know have spiritual significance.	1	3	5
7.	I find it a joy to explain to people what Jesus can do for them.	1	3	5
8.	People tell me how much they appreciate my affirmative attitude and encouraging words.	1	3	5

9.	There is no question in my mind but that God can and will often do what seems impossible.	1	3	5
10.	Knowing God will meet my need, I gladly and faithfully share my resources in response to God's love and generosity.	1	3	5
11.	I see people healed through my ministry.	1	3	5
12.	I enjoy doing work for others to free them for more important tasks.	1	3	5
13.	It is easy for me to meet guests, whether at church or in my home, and make them feel welcome and at ease.	1	3	5
14.	People come to me or phone and ask me to pray for them. They say my prayers are effectual.	1	3	5
15.	I gladly practice the disciplines of prayer and fasting so as to help others interpret their sacred experiences.	1	3	5
16.	I enjoy studying and I desire to keep my mind open to the Spirit to bless me with more light and truth.	1	3	5
17	I can recognize when a group I am in is getting its work done or progressing toward achievement of its goals.	1	3	5
18.	I enjoy being someone's spiritual adviser.	1	3	5
19.	I have a deep compassion for those who have physical or spiritual needs.	1	3	5

20. I discover myself being used as an instrument of God's power in extraordinary life changes in lives and events.	1	3	5
21. I find that I am successful as an outreach minister to people of other ethnic groups.	1	3	5
22. I enjoy being responsible for the spiritual welfare of a group of disciples and friends.	1	3	5
23. I am told how much my sermons minister to people, not just that they enjoy them.	1	3	5
24. People tell me that my presence with them is a blessing.	1	3	5
25. I have communicated timely and urgent messages to congregations and individuals that were inspired by the Holy Spirit.	1	3	5
26. I am told by members of my class how much I minister to them as a teacher.	1	3	5
27. I have been richly blessed as I have seen how people have been ministered to through my writing, music, or drama.	1	3	5
28. I am aware that God has given me aptitude in communicating with people of other nations and cultures.	1	3	5
29. I often enjoy an awareness of the Spirit's presence when important decisions	1	3	5

need to be made affecting the group I am leading.

30. I can organize ideas, people, resources, and time for more effective ministry.	1	3	5
31. I have a strong desire to extend the church into new places.	1	3	5
32. I have felt the presence of the Holy Spirit ministering to me.	1	3	5
33. I do not mind spending hours to create something of beauty that may help people glorify God.	1	3	5
34. I have little difficulty seeing the difference between truth and error.	1	3	5
35. Through the ministry of dreams and/or visions, God has used me to bring ministry to others.	1	3	5
36. Leading people to make decisions to accept and follow Jesus is one of my great joys.	1	3	5
37. I sense the need to challenge members to greater activity, service, and commitment.	1	3	5
38. I can trust the reliability of God when all looks dim.	1	3	5
39. It's a joy for me to share both Local and World Mission Tithes and other resources to support the ministry of my church in this community and throughout the world.	1	3	5

40. I am often asked to meet and pray for people who have special needs, including those that are physical in nature. 1 3 5

41. I find joy in doing what others may consider menial tasks associated with church work. 1 3 5

42. I realize great joy in providing food and/or shelter to those in need. 1 3 5

43. Praying for others is a joy to me; I never consider it a burden. 1 3 5

44. I have been able to share the meaning of the gospel cross-culturally. 1 3 5

45. At times I am blessed with insights of truth that help others to be more Christlike. 1 3 5

46. I enjoy leading in a way that enables others to feel a sense of accomplishment. 1 3 5

47. It is a joy to me to share my spiritual struggles and knowledge with a person who is seeking deeper understanding. 1 3 5

48. I enjoy visiting people in hospitals and retirement homes. 1 3 5

49. I see God miraculously changing circumstances through my ministry. 1 3 5

50. I find it rather easy to converse with people of other countries and cultures. 1 3 5

51. I find it enjoyable and challenging to relate to a group of people over a period 1 3 5

of time, sharing in their successes and failures.

52. I am willing to pay the price of serious study, fasting, prayer, and meditation to be able to give a more effective preaching ministry.	1	3	5
53. People tell me that when they are with me they feel at ease and blessed by the Spirit even though there is little, if any, talking taking place.	1	3	5
54. I am told by spiritually gifted individuals that I often have visionary insight.	1	3	5
55. One of my concerns in teaching is to teach others the truths recorded in the scriptures as well as truths revealed in other ways and places.	1	3	5
56. I sense the Spirit ministering to others when I share in one or more of the arts—drama, music, writing, etc.	1	3	5
57. I have been empowered to give important messages to people who have a different background or language from my own.	1	3	5
58. I am graced with the ability to resolve many problems.	1	3	5
59. I enjoy working with others who are responsible for various leadership roles.	1	3	5
60. One of my greatest concerns is for church expansion.	1	3	5

61. I have felt the presence of the Holy Spirit ministering through me to others. 1 3 5

62. One of the creative endeavors that blesses many people, according to what they tell me, is worship centers I set up for various church services. 1 3 5

63. More and more I am blessed with the power to see behind the masks people wear. 1 3 5

64. I sense that the gift of dreams and/or visions which I have is one of responsibility, to be dealt with in prayer. 1 3 5

65. Leading people to Jesus is a primary part of my life. 1 3 5

66. Encouraging others to be the kind of people Christ calls us to be gives me joy. 1 3 5

67. There is no doubt in my mind but that God will do all God has promised. 1 3 5

68. I enjoy the opportunity I take to increase my offerings from time to time so the church can expand its ministries in my congregation and many other places. 1 3 5

69. The Lord has seen fit to use me as an instrument in healing ministries. 1 3 5

70. I find joy and fulfillment in being a helper, rather than taking the lead. 1 3 5

71. I enjoy unexpected guests and find it easy to put them at ease. 1 3 5

72. Often I am moved by the Spirit to pray for people whom I later discover had special needs at the time of the prayer.	1	3	5
73. People contact me asking for help to interpret their life's experiences.	1	3	5
74. After prayer and study I am given fresh insights and understandings.	1	3	5
75. I enjoy leading in such a way that those who are involved feel a sense of accomplishment.	1	3	5
76. I am always ready to help those who wish to grow spiritually to develop their gifts.	1	3	5
77. I enjoy visiting and working with those who are limited in their ability to function fully.	1	3	5
78. I sense that God is using me to act as an instrument for miraculous blessings.	1	3	5
79. I enjoy a growing desire to be more involved in ethnic ministries.	1	3	5
80. I enjoy ministering in the homes of members and friends.	1	3	5
81. My preaching appears to move people of all ages to faith responses.	1	3	5
82. At times I sense that the most important ministry I can give to others is just to be with them.	1	3	5

83. There are times when I am compelled by the Spirit to speak in counsel and/or commendation.	1	3	5
84. Teaching is a joy to me as I see people expand their understanding of the meaning of life in Christ and their expressions of it.	1	3	5
85. I have a deep desire to be the best minister I can be through my music, drama, and/or writing.	1	3	5
86. I have been given the ability/aptitude to speak to highly educated groups.	1	3	5
87. I willingly pay the price of study, prayer, fasting, and meditation so I will be able to perceive and apply spiritual truth to the needs of the people when the occasion requires.	1	3	5

Gifts Identification Score Sheet

Place the numerical value of the answer you noted for each question on the Gifts Discovery Questionnaire next to the number of that question as listed. After you have all your scores listed beside the appropriate numbers, add the three scores in each set and put the total of the three on the blank line in the "Total" column. Leave the Gifts column blank for now.

Example: 1. _3_ 30. _1_ 59. _3_ = total of 7

				Total	Gifts
A	1. ____	30. ____	59. ____	______	______
B	2. ____	31. ____	60. ____	______	______

				Total	Gifts
C	3. ______	32. ______	61. ______	________	________
D	4. ______	33. ______	62. ______	________	________
E	5. ______	34. ______	63. ______	________	________
F	6. ______	35. ______	64. ______	________	________
G	7. ______	36. ______	65. ______	________	________
H	8. ______	37. ______	66. ______	________	________
I	9. ______	38. ______	67. ______	________	________
J	10. ______	39. ______	68. ______	________	________
K	11. ______	40. ______	69. ______	________	________
L	12. ______	41. ______	70. ______	________	________
M	13. ______	42. ______	71. ______	________	________
N	14. ______	43. ______	72. ______	________	________
O	15. ______	44. ______	73. ______	________	________
P	16. ______	45. ______	74. ______	________	________
Q	17. ______	46. ______	75. ______	________	________
R	18. ______	47. ______	76. ______	________	________
S	19. ______	48. ______	77. ______	________	________
T	20. ______	49. ______	78. ______	________	________
U	21. ______	50. ______	79. ______	________	________
V	22. ______	51. ______	80. ______	________	________
W	23. ______	52. ______	81. ______	________	________
X	24. ______	53. ______	82. ______	________	________
Y	25. ______	54. ______	83. ______	________	________
Z	26. ______	55. ______	84. ______	________	________
AA	27. ______	56. ______	85. ______	________	________
BB	28. ______	57. ______	86. ______	________	________
CC	29. ______	58. ______	87. ______	________	________

Now you will be able to identify your discovered gifts by following the instructions in the Gifts Discovery Report, which uses the Scriptural Definitions of Gifts resource.

Gifts Discovery Report

Now that you have totaled the score for each of the lettered categories, find your six highest scores. Refer to the Scriptural Definitions of Gifts section. Here you will find a description of the gifts used in this survey. Match the letters that are on the lines of your six highest scores with the gifts those letters identify from the Gifts Definition list. Write the titles of those six gifts in the Gifts column on the appropriate lines. List your discovered gifts in order below. You do not need to list the gift names on the remaining alphabetic lines A–Z.

Discovered Gifts:

1. ______________________________
2. ______________________________
3. ______________________________
4. ______________________________
5. ______________________________
6. ______________________________

If you have some gifts with the same high score that total more than six, carefully study your list. Decide which gifts are more apparent and useful at this time. List them according to priority. You may have a total of more than six. Remember this is a subjective self-scoring instrument that could rate you higher or lower than you really are.

Scriptural Definitions of Gifts

A. Administrative Leadership
Understands the long-range goals of a particular jurisdiction, congregation, or group, and harmonizes its activities. When this individual leads, people feel challenged and sense that their gifts are being effectively used. Broad,

long-range programs are successful as goals reached under this person's leadership.

Acts 7:10
1 Corinthians 12:28
Doctrine and Covenants 46:6

B. Apostolic Witness
Empowered with a special witness of Christ and divine direction in spiritual matters relating to church expansion. This person may be asked to assume general leadership over one or more congregations.

1 Corinthians 12:28
2 Corinthians 12:12
Galatians 2:7–10
Ephesians 3:1–9; 4:11–14
Doctrine and Covenants 148:1–2; 151:3b; 162:7a, d

C. Sensitivity to the Spirit
Empowered to sense the presence of the Holy Spirit and minister as one sent on God's behalf.

Matthew 4:11
Luke 1:11–19
John 20:11, 12
Alma 10:23, 24; 16:145, 146
Moroni 10:11
Doctrine and Covenants 67:3; 83:4c; 162:7d; 8a

D. Craftsmanship
Skilled or gifted in creating things that are beautiful and inspiring.

Exodus 35:31
Doctrine and Covenants 119:8b

E. Discernment

Able to judge between right and wrong in relation to ministerial needs and opportunities. Also, this person can discern the source or validity/divinity of the manifestations of other gifts. Some may be empowered to see and identify the spiritual gifts others have been given.

Acts 5:1–11; 16:18
1 Corinthians 12:10
1 John 4:1-6
Alma 16:51
Moroni 10:11
Doctrine and Covenants 46:7g; 162:8a

F. Dreams and Visions

Enabled by the Spirit to experience dreams and/or visions that have great significance. These may be given for personal or group ministry, including interpretation of the past, present, and future.

Joel 2:28
I Nephi 1:60
Ether 4:3

G. Evangelism

Empowered to share the good news of Jesus Christ. With this gift comes the freedom to help others choose a new life in Christ and the church.

Acts 8:5, 6; 21:8
Ephesians 4:11, 14
2 Timothy 4:5
Doctrine and Covenants 122:8c; 125:3–4; 161:3c, 6a; 162:3b, 7a, d; 8b

H. Exhortation

Has the spiritual ability to share encouragement and comfort as well as motivate toward more saintly living.

Acts 14:21–22; 20:21
Romans 12:8
1 Thessalonians 5:11
Hebrews 10:24–25
Alma 7:8–46
Doctrine and Covenants 147:2; 150:1b; 162:7a–d

I. Faith

Understands something of God's will and acts on that conviction even though the need for that action is not necessarily apparent to others. Faith is to act as if what is needed will be forthcoming.

Romans 4:19–21
1 Corinthians 12:9
Hebrews 11
Moroni 10:10
Doctrine and Covenants 34:3; 46:7; 162:7b

J. Sharing

A disciple shares generously through tithing (and at other appropriate opportunities) so that others may experience God's generosity.

Matthew 10:8
Luke 10:34–35
Luke 19:8–9
Acts 4:34–35
1 Corinthians 16:2
2 Corinthians 8:2–5, 12; 9:7
1 Timothy 6:17–19

Jacob 2:22–24
Mosiah 2:43
Alma 1:45–47
Doctrine and Covenants 59:2; 154:5a, b; 161:5; 162:7

K. Healing

Empowered to serve as an instrument through whom God can bring healing (physical, mental, psychological, spiritual, or relational) and promote wholeness of body, mind, and spirit.

Acts 3:1–10; 5:12–16; 28:7–10
1 Corinthians 12:9, 28
I Nephi 3:83–85
IV Nephi 1:6, 7
Mormon 4:66
Moroni 10:10
Doctrine and Covenants 34:3c; 46:7c; 161:2a

L. Helps

Empowered to bring enabling ministries to others. This opens the way for others to exercise their gifts and extend their ministries. It is a gift of practical support to individuals and groups.

Acts 9:36
Romans 16:1, 2
1 Corinthians 12:28

M. Hospitality

Joyfully reaches out to others (friends and strangers), offering them a warm environment of welcome and fellowship, whether at church, home, work, or any other place.

Acts 16:14–15

Romans 12:9–13
1 Peter 4:9–10
Doctrine and Covenants 161:3a–c

N. Intercessory Prayer

Empowered to pray for others for an extended period of time on a regular basis. This individual is able, through faith, to expect answers to his/her prayers and have an appreciation for the potential of this ministry.

Acts 12:12
Ephesians 1:15–19
Colossians 12:9–12
2 Thessalonians 1:11–12
1 Timothy 2:1–2
James 5:14–16
II Nephi 15:4
Words of Mormon 1:12
Moroni 8:3

O. Interpretation

Enabled by the Spirit to interpret significant experiences, and may have the ability to interpret the gospel message for other language and cultural groups.

Genesis 40
Daniel 5:1-17
1 Corinthians 12:10, 28; 14:13–19
Omni 1:44
Moroni 10:11
Doctrine and Covenants 46:7

P. Knowledge

Empowered to share the truths of the gospel. Has a continuing interest in discovering truth from the scriptures and other books, as well as life. This one is blessed with new insights, understandings, and recall of what has been studied, heard, or discussed.

1 Corinthians 2:14; 12:8
2 Corinthians 11:6
Colossians 2:2–3
II Nephi 9:117
Moroni 10:10
Doctrine and Covenants 10:7; 76:2

Q. Leadership

Empowered to develop programs and set goals that are in accordance with God's purposes. People who work with this person feel satisfied and fulfilled due to the leader's ability to communicate, create harmony, and achieve success.

Acts 8:5–6
Romans 12:8
1 Timothy 6:11
Hebrews 13:17
Doctrine and Covenants 46:8a; 119:8

R. Mentor

Has the ability to be a wise, loyal friend; a careful listener; and a spiritual adviser.

Matthew 5:1–2; 17:1–8
1 Timothy 1:1–5

S. Mercy

Enabled to give caring support through feelings of deep compassion and empathy for those who suffer, regardless of circumstances.

Matthew 25:35–36, 40/Matthew 20:29–34; 25:36–37, 41 (IV)
Luke 10:33–34 / Luke 10:34–35 (IV)
Acts 16:33–34
Romans 12:8
Galatians 2:10
Alma 7:12

T. Miracles

Empowered to be an intermediary through whom God can perform acts seen by others to be beyond the law of nature. These powerful events are often called "signs" because they point beyond themselves to the mystery of godliness.

Acts 9:32–42
Romans 15:18–19
1 Corinthians 12:10, 28
I Nephi 3:83–85
IV Nephi 1:6–7
Mormon 4:75–78
Doctrine and Covenants 34:3b–c; 83:11

U. Missionary

Divinely empowered to reach across cultures or subcultures to minister the good news of Jesus Christ.

Acts 8:4; 13:2, 3; 22:21
1 Corinthians 9:19–23
Doctrine and Covenants 151:5a; 161:3c; 162:3b, 7a

V. Pastor/Shepherd

Blessed to be able to give long-term caring support to individuals or groups. There is a sense of belonging, identity, and acceptance through his or her ministry. Such a relationship offers a deep-felt support and counsel in crisis situations.

John 10:1–18
Ephesians 4:11–12
1 Peter 5:1–3
Doctrine and Covenants 162:6c; 7a; 8b

W. Preaching
Able to preach with such insight and power that people are moved to become disciples and responsible members of the body of Christ, the church.

Acts 2:14–41; 8:5–8
Alma 7:31

X. Presence
Able to be in the presence of others and bring a blessing of the Spirit. This individual may speak only a few words, but with such quality that few words are necessary. The person's presence is the only requirement for ministry to occur.

Doctrine and Covenants 4:2; 11:4

Y. Prophecy
Empowered to receive divinely inspired insight regarding individuals and groups and to communicate it with great clarity. Ministry through this person often will be for encouragement, consolation, direction, or counsel.

Joel 2:28
Acts 15:32; 21:9–10
Romans 12:6
1 Corinthians 12:10

Ephesians 4:11–12
Jacob 3:7
Moroni 10:11
Doctrine and Covenants 46:7d

Z. Teaching
Blessed to be able to help people learn and understand principles related to the gospel.

Acts 20:20–21
Romans 12:7
1 Corinthians 12:28
Ephesians 4:11–15
Moroni 10:10
Doctrine and Covenants 85:37b

AA. The Arts (music, drama, writing)
Empowered by the Spirit (and personal preparation) to minister through any one or combination of these gifts. Those who hear or see are blessed by the Holy Spirit.

2 Chronicles 20:21, 28
Colossians 3:16
Doctrine and Covenants 119:6; 162:4a

BB. Tongues
Endowed with the unique ability to share the gospel cross-culturally. This can be through an enhanced facility with non-native languages or through the ability to use culturally appropriate metaphors and images to effectively transmit the gospel. The gift also can be one where a person is empowered to share unique insights through unfamiliar language or where a person is helped to understand a communication even thought they do not know the language of the spokesperson.

Acts 2:1–6
1 Corinthians 12:10, 28; 14:13–19
Omni 1:44
Moroni 10:11
Doctrine and Covenants 46:7e

CC. Wisdom

Endowed with insight in how knowledge or leadership may be applied to specific needs.
Acts 6:3, 10
1 Corinthians 12:8
II Nephi 9:117
Moroni 10:10
Doctrine and Covenants 46:7

Welcome Audit

1. How friendly were the people you met today?
   A. Very friendly
   B. Kind of friendly
   C. No one cared

2. Were you greeted when you walked in the door?
   A. Yes
   B. No

3. What was your first impression?
   A. I immediately felt comfortable
   B. Nervous, but not too bad
   C. Scared to death

4. Do you have friends who attend this church?
   A. Yes
   B. No
   C. Kind of

5. Have you ever been to (any) church before?
   A. Yes
   B. No

6. Did you find today's message applicable to your life?
   A. Yes
   B. No
   C. Kind of

7. Would you be open to joining a small group?
   A. Yes, please contact me
   B. No, not yet

8. Did you come with a friend or family member?
   A. Yes, I came with ______________________
   B. No

9. If you came with a friend, did they stick with you during your visit?
   A. Yes, the entire time
   B. Most of the time
   C. No, they bailed right away

10. Did you meet any of our leaders?
   A. Yes, I met________________________________
   B. No

11. How did you hear about our church?
   A. Friend
   B. Family
   C. Event flyer
   D. Web site
   E. Other________________________________

12. Would you like to join us again?
   A. Without a doubt
   B. Maybe
   C. Probably not
   D. No

13. Did you laugh at all?
   A. Yes, out loud
   B. I chuckled
   C. I was somewhat amused
   D. No, I was bored to death

   Other comments: ____________________________

Guest Survey: Welcome Barometer

1. Did you find adequate parking?
2. Was there a greeter in the parking lot?
3. Were there adequate signs directing you to the sanctuary and/or classrooms?
4. Did a greeter introduce you by name to the deacon/usher, and did the deacon/usher help you find a seat?
5. Were you introduced to other worshipers nearby?
6. Did other worshipers smile at you or greet you?
7. Were you provided with a bulletin or other information about the congregation and its programs and ministries?
8. Were you given an opportunity to register your presence on a registration form?
9. Did the person in charge of the worship service welcome visitors?
10. Did other worshipers nearby speak to you?
11. Was there an invitation for coffee or other refreshments either before or after the worship?
12. Were you offered a tour of the church facilities?
13. Did someone help you find the nursery, restrooms, sanctuary, or classrooms?
14. Did people speak to you after the worship?
15. Were visitors provided an opportunity to meet either the pastor or the person in charge of the worship?
16. Were you invited to return next Sunday?

17. Did someone ask you to be their guest and go with them to some other church function?

18. Were you or other visitors invited to join an inquirers' class?

19. What was your overall impression of your experience today?

20. Do you think that you will return to this church again?

21. Is this a place where you would invite a friend to attend?

Notes

1. Mark Ralls, "Living by the Word," *The Christian Century* 122, no. 1 (January 11, 2005):16.

2. Amy G. Oden, ed., *And You Welcomed Me: A Sourcebook on Hospitality in Early Christianity* (Nashville: Abingdon Press, 2003), 14.

3. Ibid.

4. Ibid.

5. Brendan Byrne, *The Hospitality of God: A Reading of Luke's Gospel* (Collegeville, Minnesota: The Liturgical Press, 2000), 31–32.

6. Roger K. Swanson and Shirley F. Clement, *The Faith-Sharing Congregation: Developing a Strategy for the Congregation as Evangelist* (Nashville: Discipleship Resources, 1999), 26–27.

7. Fred Bernhard and Steve Clapp, *Widening the Welcome of Your Church: Biblical Hospitality and the Vital Congregation* (Elgin, Illinois: Brethren Press, 1999), 19–20.

8. Ibid.

9. Christine D. Pohl, *Making Room: Recovering Hospitality as a Christian Tradition* (Grand Rapids, Michigan: William B. Eerdmans Publishing, 1999), 17.

10. Ibid., 25.

11. Ibid., 4.

12. Michele Hershberger, *A Christian View of Hospitality: Expecting Surprises* (Scottdale, Pennsylvania: Herald Press, 1999), 115.

13. Gary Logan, Tammy Lindle, and Eileen Terril, "Session 3: Welcoming the Stranger," from Feed My Sheep: Hospi-

tality as Lifestyle, Vibrant Witness, and Inviting Worship. Unpublished resource presented at the Congregational Leaders' Workshop, Lamoni, Iowa, August 2004. Copy in possession of author.

14. Pohl, *Making Room,* 6.
15. Hershberger, *A Christian View of Hospitality*, 114–115.
16. *Becoming a Generous Disciple: Six Principles to Live By* (Independence, Missouri: Community of Christ, 2004), 5.
17. Hershberger, *A Christian View of Hospitality*, 147.
18. *Becoming a Generous Disciple*, 5–6.
19. Oden, ed., *And You Welcomed Me*, 109–110.
20. Hershberger, *A Christian View of Hospitality*, 23–30.
21. Ibid., 24–30.
22. Henri J. M. Nouwen, *Reaching Out: The Three Movements of the Spiritual Life* (Garden City, New York: Doubleday, 1975), 47.
23. Oden, ed., *And You Welcomed Me*, 26–27.
24. Pohl, *Making Room*, 68.
25. Ibid., 174–175.
26. Megan McKenna, *Not Counting Women and Children: Neglected Stories from the Bible* (New York: Orbis Books, 1994), 23.
27. Ibid.
28. Hershberger, *A Christian View of Hospitality,* 251–252.
29. Rick Warren, *The Purpose-Driven Church: Growth without Compromising Your Message and Mission* (Grand Rapids, Michigan: Zondervan, 1995), 182.
30. Adam Hamilton, *Leading beyond the Walls: Developing Congregations with a Heart for the Unchurched* (Nashville: Abingdon Press, 2002), 38.

31. Russell Chandler, *Feeding the Flock: Restaurants and Churches You'd Stand in Line For* (Bethesda, Maryland: the Alban Institute, 1998), 5–6.

32. Adapted from Karen Risch, ed. *Beyond 30 Seconds: Developing a Welcoming Congregation: A Seven-Session Video Curriculum* (Nashville: United Methodist Communications, 2003), 1.4.

33. Hershberger, *A Christian View of Hospitality,* 252–253.

34. Lee Strobel, *Inside the Mind of Unchurched Harry and Mary: How to Reach Friends and Family Who Avoid God and the Church* (Grand Rapids, Michigan: Zondervan, 1993), 161.

35. Andrew Bolton and Jane Gardner, eds. *The Sacraments: Symbol, Meaning, and Discipleship* (Independence, Missouri: Herald House, 2005), 68.

36. Ginny Thornburgh, ed. *That All May Worship: An Interfaith Welcome to People With Disabilities* (Washington, D.C.: National Organization on Disability, 1992), 10–11.

37. Ibid., 15.

38. Linda L. Pickens-Jones, *Along the Way: Meeting God and Neighbor in Unexpected Places* (Nashville: Abingdon Press, 2000), 52.

39. Nouwen, *Reaching Out*, 46.

40. Hershberger, *A Christian View of Hospitality*, 21.

41. *Luther's Works* (Philadelphia: Fortress, 1955), vol. 4, "Lectures on Genesis Chapters 21–25," 282; vol. 3, "Lectures on Genesis Chapters 15–20," 245. (As quoted in Pohl, *Making Room*, 93–94.)

42. Pohl, *Making Room*, 127–128.

43. Oden, ed. *And You Welcomed Me*, 132–133.

44. Gary Logan, Tammy Lindle, and Eileen Terril, "Session 4: Open Heart, Open Home," Feed My Sheep: Hospitality as Lifestyle, Vibrant Witness, and Inviting Worship. Unpublished resource presented at the Congregational Leaders' Workshop, 2004.

45. Jean Vanier, *Community and Growth*, rev. ed. (New York: Paulist Press, 2001), 179–180.

46. Adapted from Vanier, *Community and Growth*, 165.

47. Nouwen, *Reaching Out*, 70.

48. Oden, ed. *And You Welcomed Me*, 147.

49. Philip Hallie, *Tales of Good and Evil, Help and Harm* (New York: HarperCollins, 1997), 42. (As quoted in Christine D. Pohl, *Making Room: Recovering Hospitality as a Christian Tradition* (Grand Rapids, Michigan: William B. Eerdmans Publishing, 1999), 14.)

50. Swanson and Clement. *The Faith-Sharing Congregation*, 31.

51. Nouwen, *Reaching Out*, 87. (As quoted in Pohl, *Making Room*, 180.)

52. Pohl, *Making Room*, 58.

53. Excerpted from Susan Eaton Mendenhall, "Can Churches Become a Third Place for Community?" *Net Results* (March/April, 2006), 26.

54. Adapted from John T. Conway, Harry L. Doty, Roy H. Schaefer, *Discover and Share Your Gifts* (Independence, Missouri: Herald House, 1994), 20–29.